MOUNTAIN BIKE GUIDE

COTSWOLDS

Nick Cotton

Cordee – Leicester

Regional Map

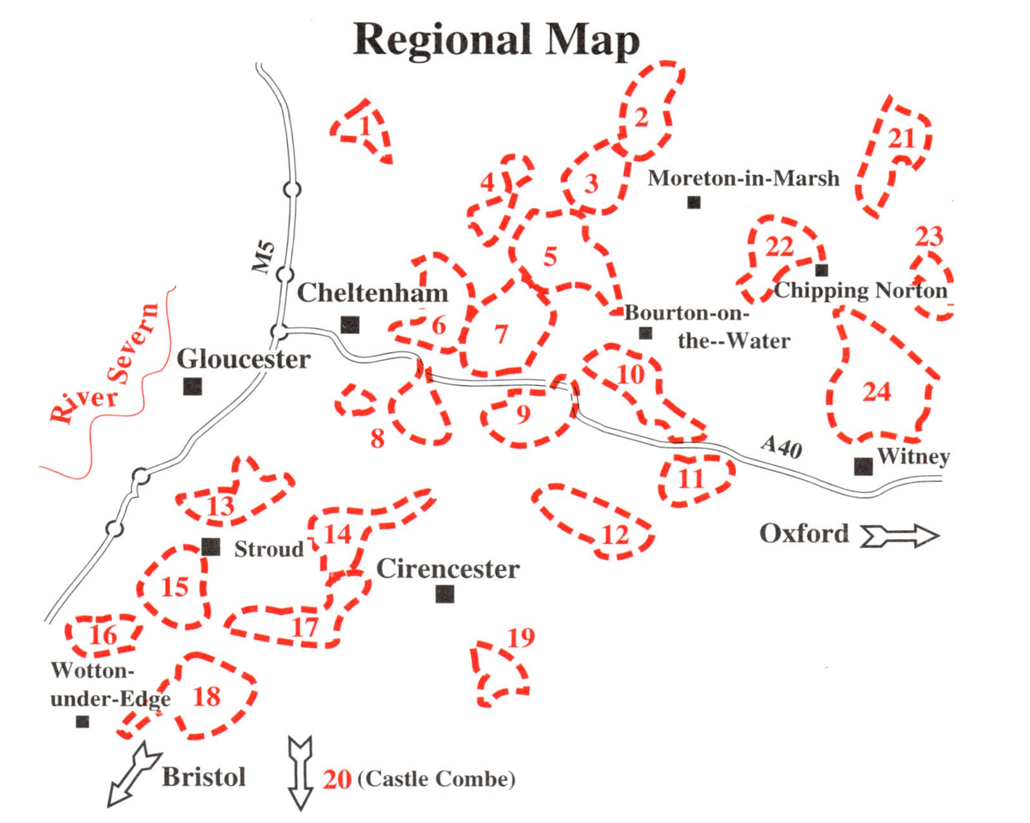

Contents

ISBN 1 871890 17 9

British Library Cataloguing in Publication Data
A catalogue record for this book is available from the British Library

All trade enquiries to:
Cordee, 3a De Montfort Street, Leicester LE1 7HD

All photographs by the author. Cover: Excellent all-weather track between Cold Aston and Hazleton, close to Turkdean. Rear cover: View northeast from Cam Long Down towards Coaley Peak.

This book is available from all specialist equipment shops and major booksellers. It can, along with all the maps mentioned in the text be obtained direct from the publishers. Please write for a copy of our comprehensive stocklist of mountain bike guides and other outdoor recreation books/maps.

▬ ▬ ▬ ▬ ▬ ▬	**Route**
═══════	**Road**
• • • • • • • • • • • •	**Track may be muddy in winter/after rain**
+++++++++	**Alternative route to avoid mud**
❯	**Steep Climb**
☀	**Fine views**
✳	**Good descent**
🍺	**Public house**
▲	**High points**
Banbury ⇨	**Nearby towns/villages**

Introduction

The geography

The physical geography of the Cotswolds consists of a long relatively steep scarp face extending south-westwards from Mickleton near Stratford-Upon-Avon to Wotton-under-Edge and the countryside north of Bath. This scarp has splendid views out over the Avon and Severn valleys. Behind the edge, the hills to its east consist largely of open wold country — the Cotswolds' best known feature. Here were the great sheep runs of the Middle Ages, later divided up by long dry-stone walls erected largely during the 18th and 19th centuries, the time of the enclosures, and also relieved by the scattered beech plantations of the great enclosing landlords. These walls and woodlands still endure. The northern half of this area, between Chipping Campden and Winchcombe consists of wide, rolling country with many distant views and broad open skies. It lies largely within the Thames watershed and few streams of any consequence flow north or west to join the Avon or Severn.

Further south, beyond Cheltenham, the character of much of the hill country changes considerably. Here are deep, often densely wooded valleys, some carrying streams flowing south to the Thames and others feeding the Severn, largely via the deeply intruding valley of the River Frome. This was the country that gave birth to the great cloth industries of the 17th, 18th and early 19th centuries.

To the east of these wooded valleys, beyond Tetbury and Cirencester, and further eastwards to Bibury and Burford, the character of the countryside is closer to that of the northern Cotswolds, with its open wold country here intersected by a series of delightful clear-watered streams flowing southwards to the Thames. The area's southern extremities merge with the flat gravel country of the Upper Thames Valley, and beyond Burford, to the east, lie the the remains of the great forest of Wychwood.

The towns and villages amongst these hills are enriched by some of the loveliest medieval churches and domestic buildings to be found anywhere in Britain and it is the combination of the geography and the architecture that gives the Cotswolds its unique flavour.

The history

Being comparatively easy to cultivate, Cotswold limestone provided Stone Age man with ideal farming country. Having arrived from continental Europe, by 2500 BC the early settlers had firmly established themselves on the upland ridges of the Cotswolds. About 2000 BC, the arrival of the Beaker Folk heralded the start of the Bronze Age. They worshipped at stone circles or henges such as the modestly sized Rollright Stones which are situated close to the line of one of Britain's great prehistoric trade routes – the Jurassic Way. A third wave of settlers, the Belgic, Iron Age settlers moved westward around 500 BC. this last bunch were responsible amongst other earthmoving extravaganzas for Uleybury and the fort on Haresfield Beacon.

The Romans landed in AD 43 and soon had advanced as far as a line that was later to become the Foss Way. A provincial capital was established at Cirencester and a network of roads was developed around it: the Foss Way, the Ermin Way, Akeman Street and the White Way. By AD 577, the Anglo-Saxons had conquered Gloucester and Cirencester and the Dark Ages were upon the land. After 1066, the Normans were the final invaders to come across the channel, land in the east and make their way westwards. The Cotswolds are particularly rich in Norman churches: routes pass near to fine examples in Avening, Windrush, Hook Norton and Quenington.

The period from the late 14th to the early 16th century was an age of great prosperity, with sheep graziers, wool merchants and clothiers amassing considerable wealth. The wool merchants spent generously and we are indebted to them for the great 'wool' churches of Cirencester, Chipping Campden, Northleach and Wotton-Under-Edge.

Following Henry VIII's dissolution of the abbeys in 1539, their great wealth passed into the hands of noble families, merchants and other lay landowners who built the series of fine 16th and 17th century manor houses and mansions and the lovely villages often to be found at their gates. The 18th century produced an even greater number of fine houses and parks, in many cases created as a result of the acceleration of the enclosures, a process begun in the 16th century and largely completed by the 19th, the fruit of the changes in agricultural methods now known collectively as the Agricultural Revolution.

By contrast, the Cotswolds were hardly touched by the Industrial Revolution, although the 18th and 19th centuries saw the flowering of a great cloth industry in the deep valleys of the south-west around Stroud and

Dursley. This activity was gathered into factories, first water-powered and later driven by steam. The Stroudwater Canal and the Thames and Severn Canal were established at this time, but then slowly faded as the railways were developed. The cloth industry was overwhelmed by the competition from the northern industrial towns.

The coming of the railways in the mid-19th century sent the hitherto robust coaching inns (typified by those at Burford) into a state of hibernation from which they only began to awake in the 1930's. At the end of the 20th century, the railways face the same fate as the canals of an earlier age: the single track line following the Evenlode Valley to Moreton-in-Marsh and beneath the hills of Chipping Campden, together with the line from Swindon to Stroud represents all that is left of the network that used to serve the Cotswolds. If only Beeching had been a cyclist......

Cotswold Stone

The great limestone belt of hills stretching from the Humber to the Dorset coast of which the Cotswolds form a part, contains many different varieties of stone. All Cotswold stone is known as oolite (egg-stone), being composed of small, rounded, egg-shaped grains, but it is found in several forms.

Usually close to the surface is the stone used for dry stone walling, most of which was built in the time of the enclosures in the 18th and 19th centuries. Some beds of oolitic limestone are in thin layers, which are suitable for splitting into roofing tiles by exposure to frost. The best-known source was in great caverns beneath Stonesfield, near Charlbury. They are graded in size on almost all Cotswold roofs, with the biggest tiles at the bottom of the roof weighing up to 50 lbs, gradually becoming smaller towards the ridge. Each size of tile had a different name and including wacky ones as 'Short Bachelor', 'Muffity' and 'Short Cock'.

The third type of stone is known as freestone, so called because it is easy to work when newly quarried. It hardens on exposure to the elements and soon harmonises with its surroundings. It is found in many different shades, from the golden in the Bath area, through the grey whites of Painswick to the honey colour of Broadway and Chipping Campden and the tawny brown iron-stone of the Oxfordshire hills. Easy working enabled Cotswold masons to produce far more interesting architectural detail than would otherwise have been possible – mullions, transoms, drip mouldings, gargoyles, church crosses and porches, to name just a few.

Because of transport difficulties stone was normally quarried locally to fulfil most needs, but from the later Middle Ages Cotswold stone was also being used for buildings in London, Windsor and Oxford, to which it was carried on barges down the Thames. Most of the stone for this purpose was quarried in the Windrush Valley at Upton, near Burford and the nearby villages of Taynton, Great and Little Barrington and Windrush. Much of this was obtained from conventional open quarries, but that from the Windrush was 'mined' by driving passages similar to those at Stonesfield into the nearby hill-slopes. Today only a small amount of Cotswold stone is extracted from the hills, with most new houses being built with reconstituted stone and roofed with moulded tiles.

Environment and code of conduct

While accepting that riding in the Cotswolds presents neither the environmental dilemmas nor the same degree of conflict of interest between walkers and cyclists as somewhere like the Lake District or Snowdonia, the underlying principles remain the same.

Mountain bikers are newcomers to the scene. Cyclists have only had the right to use bridleways in the last 25 years and this on condition that we give way to walkers and horseriders. Think of yourself as a Billy Graham of mountain biking! Let people have faith in the good sense and good nature of mountain bikers and mountain biking. Show courtesy, say hello, take special care not to frighten horses, this best achieved by a hearty 'Hallooo' rather than whooshing past without warning. Avoid cutting up soft grass, show that we care as much about sharing the joys of the outdoors as any other group. You will not only make it easy for yourself if you come across the same people again, you are doing a real favour to all other mountain bikers who may use the same track at a later stage and come across these walkers/ horseriders. Try to avoid cycling in groups larger than 5-6. The bigger the group, the more effort you should make with other people you may meet, as a large group can appear somewhat threatening.

There are two codes of conduct relevant to mountain biking:

The Off Road Code issued by the Mountain Bike Club.

Only ride where you know you have a legal right.
Always yield to horses and pedestrians.
Avoid animals and crops. In some circumstances this may not be possible, at which times contact should be kept to a minimum.
Take all litter with you.
Leave all gates as found.
Keep the noise down.
Don't get annoyed with anyone, it never solves any problems.
Always try to be self-sufficient, for you and your bike.
Never create a fire hazard.

The Country Code issued by the Countryside Commission.

Enjoy the countryside and respect its life and work.
Guard against all risk of fire.
Fasten all gates.
Keep your dogs under close control.
Keep to public paths across farmland.
Use gates and stiles to cross fences, hedges and walls.
Leave livestock, crops and machinery alone.
Take your litter home.
Help keep all water clean.
Protect wildlife, plants and trees.
Take special care on country roads.
Make no unnecessary noise.

Maps and Rights of Way

The 1968 Wildlife and Countryside Act gave cyclists the right to cycle on bridleways, on condition that they give way to pedestrians and horse riders. While at present there is no right to cycle on a footpath, the law relating to pushing a bike along a footpath is murky in the extreme. There is no question about your right to be there as an individual, the question centres around the right of your bicycle to be there! In addition to bridleways, cyclists are also allowed to ride on Roads Used as Public Paths (RUPPs) and Byways Open to All Traffic (BOATs).

There are three other areas which are of interest to cyclists seeking to escape traffic, although only the last of these is relevant to this book.

1. Forestry Commission land. Most Forestry Commissions are adopting ever more liberal views about the use by mountain bikes on tracks in the land they administer. The nearest large area with this status is the Forest of Dean.

2. British Waterways Canal Towpaths. The area nearest to the Cotswolds is covered by the British Waterways offices in Gloucester. The nearest towpaths are alongside the Gloucester and Sharpness Canal in the Severn Vale and the Kennet and Avon Canal from Bath to Reading.

3. Unclassified county roads, class 4, 5 and 6. These may vary from a tarmac road that is gradually falling into disrepair right down to a mere hint that something once existed. These are public roads, maintained at public expense, but so far the Ordnance Survey has not come up with a way of showing them on maps which distinguishes them from private drives or private farm tracks. Both private and public tend to be marked on the maps as 'white roads' or black dashes and it is only by phoning or writing a letter to the Rights of Way Department at the County Council of the relevant area, quoting grid number references, that you will find whether you have a right of way or not. They will consult the 'Definitive Maps' or a map showing all the county roads at a scale of 1:10,000 and will be able to throw light on the subject. Alternatively you may wish to turn up personally at the Rights of Way Department with your own maps in order to highlight the unclassified roads. Some of the routes in this book use these unclassified roads.

Complaints about the Rights of Way system

As you wander about the countryside on your bike you may come across the odd problem that sends you reaching for your pen. The 'problem' at its most serious would be that you were being threatened by a landowner when you had a perfectly legal right to be there. Try not to get angry but refer the incident to the Rights of Way Department as soon as possible. Similarly if you find locked gates or obstructions on routes open to cyclists.

In the case of the bridleway/byway being in a distressingly muddy or overgrown state, the budgets of any Rights of Way Department are severely limited, but they do tend to give priority to letters, particularly if several people refer to the same problem. With concerted action a lot can be achieved. When writing the letter try to be as specific as possible, giving grid references and stating the nature of the problem.

The Cotswolds as covered by this book fall within six counties, although almost all the routes are situated in Gloucestershire and Oxfordshire. The addresses of the Rights of Way Departments are as follows:

Gloucestershire County Council,
County Surveyors Department,
Bearland,
Shire Hall,
Gloucester.
GL1 2TH

Oxfordshire County Council,
Department of Leisure and Arts Countryside Service,
Holton,
Oxford.
OX33 1QQ

Warwickshire County Council,
Planning and Transport Dept.,
PO Box 43,
Shire Hall,
Warwick.
CV34 4SX

Wiltshire County Council, Dept. of Planning and Highways,
County Hall,
Trowbridge,
Wiltshire BA14 8JD.

Avon and Worcestershire are not included in this list, as the rights of way on Bredon Hill (Route 1, Worcester) and near Ozleworth (Route 18, Avon) fall within the Cotswold Area of Outstanding Natural Beauty and are maintained by the Cotswold Wardens at Gloucester.

List of routes and the counties (or administration) within which they fall:

1. Bredon (Glos)
2. Chipping Campden (Glos + Warks)
3. Blockley (Glos)
4. Stanton (Glos)
5. Upper Slaughter (Glos)
6. Winchcombe (Glos)
7. Naunton (Glos)
8. Andoversford (Glos)
9. Northleach (Glos)
10. Bourton-on-the-Water (Glos + Ox)
11. Burford (Glos + Ox)
12. Bibury (Glos)
13. Painswick (Glos)
14. Bisley (Glos)
15. Stonehouse (Glos)
16. Cam Long Down (Glos)
17. Nailsworth (Glos)
18. Leighterton (Glos + Avon)
19. Cotswold Water Pk (Glos + Wilts)
20. Castle Combe (Wilts)
21. Hook Norton (Ox)
22. Chipping Norton (Ox + Glos + Warks)
23. Great Tew (Ox)
24. Stonesfield (Ox)
25. The Forest of Dean (Glos)

Addresses and accommodation

It would be an unenviable task to list and recommend accommodation in the Cotswold area. There is plenty of choice at all levels from campsites to top quality hotels. Instead of individual recommendations you will find a list of the Tourist Information Centres in the area: they tend to be very helpful and most of them offer a service of booking accommodation on your behalf for a small charge, once they know what you are looking for.

If all else fails, the Post Office in the smaller towns and villages, the number of which can be found via Directory Enquiries, usually knows who offers accommodation in the area, or they may put you in contact with the local pub who will also know where you can stay. The more well-known the area, the more expensive the prices, but the greater choice on offer, both for accommodation and places to eat.

Tourist Information Centres

Bath, The Colonnades, 11-13 Bath Street. (0225) 462831.
Broadway, 1 Cotswold Court. (0386) 852937
Burford, The Brewery, Sheep Street. (0993) 823558
Cheltenham, Municipal Offices, 77 The Promenade. (0242) 522878
Chipping Campden, Woolstaplers Hall, High Street. (0386) 840289 or 840101
Chipping Norton, New Street Car Park. (0608) 644379
Cirencester, Corn Hall, Market Place. (0285) 654180
Northleach, The Cotswold Countryside Museum. (0451) 60715
Painswick, Painswick Library. (0452) 813552
Stow-on-the-Wold, Talbot Court. (0451) 831082
Stroud, Subscription Rooms. (0453) 765768
Tetbury, The Old Court House, 63 Long Street. (0666) 503552.
Tewkesbury, 64 Barton Street. (0684) 295027
Winchcombe, Town Hall. (0242) 602925
Woodstock, Hensington Road. (0993) 811038.

Bike shops

As with accommodation, no attempt is made to recommend individual bike shops. The larger the town/city the greater the choice. Within the area, you will find bike shops in the following places:

Banbury	Bath	Bourton-on-the-Water
Chalford	Cheltenham	Chipping Norton
Cirencester	Evesham	Gloucester
Malmesbury	Moreton in Marsh	Oxford
Stow-on-the-Wold	Stroud	Tetbury
Tewkesbury	Witney	Wotton-Under-Edge

The bike and what to take with you

Preparing the bike

This book does not aim in any way to be a maintenance manual. There are plenty of these on the market that will take you step by step through the grime and delights of repairing and servicing your own bike. If you have no time or inclination to do anything about it yourself, get friendly with your local bike shop and give them plenty of time to repair/service the bike ready for when you need it.

Most advice about preparing your bike for the sort of riding involved in touring the Cotswolds is common sense.

If you are planning a ride at the weekend, do not leave it until the last moment before checking to see if your bike is fit to leap on to and go. Bikes have a habit of inducing amnesia the moment you finish a ride, making you forget those niggly little things that made your bike's performance less than 100% . It is not only a pain in the backside for you to be fiddling about with your bike on the day of the ride, it is also irritating for anyone else going out with you.

BRAKES. Do your brakes work efficiently without squealing? Adjusting or changing brake blocks is a job often more easily done with two people and four hands. Change brake blocks that are close to the end of their lives for new ones, as brake blocks worn down to the metal do serious damage to the rims of the wheels, which are a lot more expensive to replace than brake blocks. Changing brake cables is very cheap, easy and can make an enormous difference to stiff brake levers.

Squirting spray lube on any moving part never did any harm. Carrying a spare set of blocks is no bad idea, particularly on wet days when the rubber blocks can wear very quickly.

TYRES. Because of the nature of offroad riding, it is very easy to pick up thorns that do not immediately cause punctures, but lie embedded in the tyre and may cause a slow puncture from one ride to the next. Check the tyre pressure the day before the ride and if it is even the slightest bit softer than when you were last out, take off the tyre, blow up the tube in a bowl of water and look out for the tiniest of bubbles coming from a small puncture. MOST IMPORTANT. Check the inside of the tyre, very slowly and carefully moving your fingers along the inside to feel if there are any thorns sticking through. This is essential. Use a screwdriver/tweezers to winkle out any thorns.

Some rims seem to have a habit of chewing up the sidewalls of tyres. If your wheel feels as though it has gone out of true, but the rim is not bent and there are no broken spokes, check to see if the tyre sidewall is bulging at any point. Change the tyre.

GEARS. Although not as essential to check as brakes and tyres, gears that work sweetly are a real joy and gears that don't are miserable. If you need to adjust your gears, set aside a little time as you need to work by trial and error. The faults most likely to be occurring are that the chain is coming off the front or back cogs, either away from the frame or towards the frame, OR the chain is failing to move across on to the largest or smallest cogs, front or rear. There are (at least!) eight different problems here. Tightening or loosening one of the two small grub screws on either the front or the rear derailleur will increase or decrease the chain's range of sideways movement. Do this GRADUALLY and go for a short ride after each quarter turn of the screw to check to see if you have made the problem worse or better.

Gear changes which were once crisp can become sloppy. The cable has probably stretched and needs to be tightened via the barrel adjuster at the back of the rear derailleur. As with brakes, lubricating all moving parts always helps.

BEARINGS. It is possible to live for a while with loose or worn bearings in the areas which contain them: front and rear hubs, headset, bottom bracket, pedals and freewheel BUT it is not very clever. A bottom bracket or a pedal seizing up in the middle of nowhere is no fun and loose/worn bearings tend to wear the more expensive parts far more quickly. Bearings themselves cost very little. Changing them can take time.

LUBRICATION. Lubricant manufacturers tend to make extravagant claims about their own products being far better than those of their rivals. Well they would wouldn't they? When your bike is about to go through water and mud, ANY lubricant is better than none, and I have never found that you can OVER lubricate a bike when it is going to be used offroad. The best way is to tip/lie the bike on one side and lubricate hubs, bottom bracket, brakes, pedals and gear mechanisms on one side, then tip it the other way and do the other side. Pay special attention to the chain which will need something denser than a spray lubricant. If there are a few of you on a ride or you are planning a long day out, it is probably worth taking a small oilcan with a screwtop.

What to take with you:

(A) TOOLS

The absolute minimum is a pump and a puncture repair kit. A puncture can happen any time, anywhere and if you DON'T have the above it will happen at the furthest point from the start, Sod's Law. The following are suggestions if you are somewhere between the minimalist and the kitchen sinker:

pump, puncture repair kit, spare inner tube, tyre levers (many mountain bike tyres can be removed without tyre levers)
reversible screw driver, small adjustable spanner, allen keys
chain link extractor, spare set of brake blocks.

For extended touring:

spare brake and gear cables (rear ones can always be shortened to fit the front)
cone spanners, freewheel extractor, spoke key, spare spokes, crank extractor, headset spanner, small pliers.
small oil can, length of soft wire, strong fabric tape.

(B) CLOTHES AND BAGS

The aim is to be warm, dry and comfortable, to wear clothes you won't worry about getting covered in mud and to carry any tools/spare gear/food in a way that doesn't detract from enjoying the ride.

Upper body: thermal top / fleece keep you warm and wick away the moisture. Wool keeps you warm even when wet. A Goretex cycling top is long at the back and short at the front and designed for freedom of movement. It is also expensive. In extremis, a black bin liner with holes punched through for head and arms would keep you from getting drenched or chilled by the wind! A hat and scarf for fine tuning of temperature control. Gloves both for warmth and for padding for your hands on the downhills. Sunglasses in the unlikely event of sun or the more likely event of midges. I sincerely hope that the wearing of helmets remains a matter of personal choice.

Legs: padded cycling shorts DO make a tremendous improvement in comfort. If you wouldn't be seen dead in lycra, there are padded shorts which fit under ordinary clothes. Stretch leggings or Tracksters are by far the most comfortable form of leg covering, and together with thermal bottoms can cope with some fairly extreme weather. Tight non-stretch fabrics like denim make cycling very hard work, normally have seams in the wrong place and are hopeless when wet. Baggy tracksuit bottoms hold gallons of water, tend to sag and may well get caught in the chain. It is usually advisable to have some sort of covering on both arms and legs even in the summer as you are likely to come across tracks with vegetation that could bite you!

Feet: you may opt for a £150 combination of SPD shoes and pedals. You may choose wellies and no toe clips. Strong cases could be made for either. Whatever you decide, be aware that your footwear could be covered in mud by the end of the ride.

Panniers/backpacks/hip belts (bum bags): even if you go for the minimalist approach you will need somewhere to put an inner tube and a few tools. Try using either a small hip belt/bumbag or a tool pouch that fits under the saddle. If you are carrying a waterproof/food/extra clothes you will need to consider a small daypack, panniers or (my preference) a small top bag that sits on top of a back rack, making the bike no wider, nor restricting your movement.

(C) NAVIGATION

It would be nice to think that you need no more than the instructions in this book, but realistically you should always carry an OS map of the area in case you get lost or need to change your plans because of tiredness, breakdown or deterioration in the weather. It is highly advisable either to buy laminated maps or to laminate them yourself as they disintegrate rapidly in wet, muddy conditions. Map holders are useful, whether slung over the shoulder or mounted on the handlebars. (The VK map holder, a Dutch design, is the best mounted holder I have found). Taking a compass in conjunction with a map makes sense, not because you are ever in extreme exposed conditions in the Cotswolds, but if you are ever in doubt in woodland or at a fork/junction of tracks it is reassuring to confirm that you are headed in the right direction.

(D) FOOD AND DRINK

This book describes touring, not racing, so as with all the above advice, common sense is the basic guideline. On many of the rides you will come across pubs or shops where you can buy refreshments. It is always wise, however, to carry water with you, as you can quickly dehydrate on a hot day and/or on a strenuous ride. Bottle cages holding bottles tend to get covered in mud so it is often better to put the bottle in a pack/pannier. As for emergency food, dried fruit and nuts give lots of energy and don't melt/go stale. Recent surveys have shown that a pot of tea and bread pudding or malt loaf give your body almost as many of the vital ingredients you need before or after hard exercise as the most expensive products!
(Ie – water and complex carbohydrates)

(E) OTHER SUNDRIES.

Money helps in pubs and shops. A 20p coin can let you make that phone call to ask for help (the frame has broken /a wheel has collapsed) or to let someone know that you will be back later than expected.

Lights. If you are riding on roads after dark you will need front and rear lights. If you are riding offroad at night there are some very good, very expensive lighting systems or the Petzl head torches are a useful alternative. A reflector belt / reflective ankle strips help you to be seen.

Lock. If you are going to leave your bike for any length of time, LOCK IT!

Camera and film? Make sure it is well protected against water, mud and vibration as you bounce downhill.

Bin liners left in the car are useful for all that muddy kit. Carry some spare clothes/footwear to change into. Along the same lines, extra food and/or a thermos of something hot is always welcome at the end of a ride.

Directions explained

Most of this is straightforward: you will find three instructions in bold type:

R – right
RH – right hand
L – left
LH – left hand
SA – straight ahead or straight across.

These are instructions you need to follow to continue the route. Where you see 'right' or 'left' or 'ahead' written in full it is to indicate the position of a waymark or a building or some other feature to give you a bearing ie 'shortly after passing church on your left, take next R'

There are four types of right (or left) turns:

'bear R, in effect SA' – you leave the road/track as it swings around to the left, carrying on in the same direction in which you have been travelling.

'bear R' or 'diagonally R' – you leave the road/track at an angle equivalent to 1 or 2 o'clock on a clock face.

'R' or 'turn R' – may well refer to what you have to do at a T-junction or a crossroads ie normally a 90° turn.

'sharply R, back on yourself' – you leave the road/track at an angle equivalent to 4 or 5 o'clock on a clock face.

Other abbreviations

T-j – T-junction
x-rds – crossroads

Signposting

What is written on a signpost is indicated by quote marks ie 'Chipping Campden 3, Stow-on-the-Wold 6'

If there is a signpost with a white horse or with the words 'Bridleway' or 'Public Bridleway' they are shown in the text as 'Public Bridleway' ie no distinction is made between these three forms of waymarking.

Occasionally blue arrows are used to indicate the course of a bridleway, in which case they are mentioned as such.

Other information

Without signposts it is at times difficult to explain which of several options should be taken, particularly in woodland, which may change anyway as forestry work is undertaken or from one season to the next. Hence attention should be paid to details such as 'slightly uphill on broad track'. This may well distinguish the chosen track from others that are narrow, flat or downhill.

Wet weather alternatives

In the winter or after a spell of wet weather, some parts of some of the routes will become hard going as the famous Cotswold mud rears its ugly head. Occasionally routes may run across or along the edge of fields which are annually ploughed. For a short time after ploughing these sections will be almost impossible to use until the farmer re-establishes the course of the right of way. It is difficult to say how far into autumn/winter or after how much rain the routes change from being a bit rough to very unpleasant, but where possible I have suggested (quiet) road alternatives to minimise the mud you have to go through. It is entirely at your own discretion to choose the road/offroad options and in some cases you may have to devise your own alternative to an offroad section that, despite my research, proves to be inappropriate for cycling at the time you do the route. Another overwhelming reason to take an OS map with you.

Route	Distance Grade	Links/ nearby routes	Mud factor	Fine day views	OS maps	Page no.
1 Bredon Hill	10 miles Moderate		Low	Yes	LR 150	29
2 Chipping Campden	17 miles Moderate	3	Low		LR 151	33
3 Blockley	11 miles Moderate	2 4 5	Low		LR 150,151 PF 1043	37
4 Stanton	17 miles Strenuous	3 5 6 7	Low·	Yes	LR 150	41
5 Upper Slaughter	18 miles Moderate	3 4 7	Medium (* Alt)		LR 150,151,163 PF 1043,1067	45
6 Winchcombe	16 miles Mod/stren	4 5 7 8	Medium (* Alt)		LR 163	49
7 Naunton	20 miles Moderate	4,5 8,9 10	Medium		LR 163	53
8 Andovers- ford	16 or 24 Strenuous	6 7	Medium /high	Yes	LR 163	57

9 Northleach	17 miles Moderate	7 8 10 12	Low		LR 163	63
10 Bourton on-the- Water	19 miles Moderate	5 7 9 11	High (* Alt)		LR 163	67
11 Burford	15 miles Easy/mod OR 10 miles Easy	10 12	Medium (* Alt) Low		LR163	71
12 Bibury	19 miles Easy	9 11	Medium		LR 163	75
13 Painswick	18 miles Strenuous	14	Medium	Yes	LR 162,163 PF 1089,1113	79
14 Bisley	20 miles Strenuous	13 17	Medium		LR 163	83
15 Stonehouse	13 miles Moderate	16 17 18	Medium		LR 162	87

(The Stonehouse-Nailsworth cyclepath is flat and ideal for families)

16 Cam Long Down	13 miles Strenuous	15 18	High	Yes	LR 162 PF 1132	91
17 Nailsworth	19 miles Mod/stren	14 15 18	Medium (* Alt)		LR 162,163 PF 1113,1133	95

No.	Location	Distance	Alt	Traffic	Maps	Page
18	Leigh-terton	20 miles Mod/stren	15 16 17	High (* Alt)	LR 162 PF 1132,1133	99
19	Cotswold Water Park	9 miles Very Easy		Low	LR 163	103
20	Castle Combe	15 miles Moderate		High	LR 173	107
21	Hook Norton	17 miles Moderate	22	Medium (* Alt)	LR 151	111
22	Chipping Norton	18 miles Moderate	21 24	Medium (* Alt)	LR 151,163,164 PF 1044,1068	115
23	Great Tew	10 miles Easy	24	Low	LR 164	119
24	Stones-field	24 miles Moderate	23	Medium	LR 164	123

Grades

Giving grades to offroad routes is notoriously difficult, not only because of differing levels of fitness from one person to another but also because of the effect that the weather and seasons have on the going underfoot (under wheel!). I have deliberately avoided indicating the length of time a route may take as there may be a difference of up to 50% from winter to summer. In fact, some rides are almost impossible in the depths of a wet winter. In reasonable conditions it should be possible to average 5-6 miles an hour for most of the routes, meaning that most will take 3-4 hours if cycled non-stop.

Links

With the above in mind, rather than put together any 50 mile challenges for superstars, I have indicated where there are routes which may link easily to form longer, harder rides. The best way to link two rides is either to start at a point where they touch/are at their closest and do the rides sequentially OR to do half of one ride, leave it to hop over to the other ride, do the second ride in its entirety then return to the first ride to finish off the last part. The advantage of this system is that you can make up your mind during the course of the ride according to how you feel and what the conditions are whether you want to extend your planned trip. By careful study of the relevant OS maps you should be able to figure out where the best links are to be made.

Mud factor

As mentioned in the introduction, mud is a major player in offroad cycling in the Cotswolds. During a very wet winter, many of the tracks become all but impassable because mud coats the wheels in a sticky gloop which starts picking up leaves and twigs and eventually prevents the wheels from turning. If you live in an area of acidic, peaty soils or in granite or carboniferous limestone country, you are lucky in this respect and it may be an eye opener to see how the quality of the soil in large areas of southern England affects the quality of the ride.

With this as a nightmare I have tried not only to avoid the worst trouble spots when devising the routes but also to find road alternatives (* Alt) where there is a likelihood that the mud would prove to be a real problem in winter/after rain. In certain cases this has not been possible so I would advise leaving a route with a 'High' mud factor and no suggested road alternatives to the late spring onwards and preferably after a few dry days. In many cases I have contacted the relevant local authority with details of any problem sections. It would be enormously helpful if you would do the same, in a letter, giving the grid reference of the area in question and stating the nature of the problem. Gloucestershire, which has the lion's share of the routes described in this book, has a fairly dynamic Rights of Way team and seem responsive to constructive suggestions.

The other obvious point to make about the mud is that you should be prepared to see your footwear caked in the stuff. Although it does not have much street cred with the lycra and shades boys, much of my winter riding is done in wellies. Cost? About a fiver. Mud over your ankles? No problem. Cleaning? Try a jet hose.

Fine day views

Most of the routes have good views at some point during their course. Some have spectacular views that really are best appreciated on a day of good visibility. This is not necessarily a hot summer's day when a heat haze may build up. Visibility is often best on a bright day when there are big fluffy clouds in a blue sky. The routes with the very best views are those that peer westards over the escarpment from Painswick or Birdlip or Bredon.

Maps

The routes described in this book are covered by six Ordnance Survey Landranger maps, numbers 150, 151, 162, 163, 164 and 173. The scale on these is 1:50,000 or 1¼ inches to the mile (2 cms to 1 kilometre). This is normally sufficient, but in certain circumstances, for example in woodland or near the escarpment where greater detail is required OR where the route is on two or even three Landranger maps, it may well be preferable to use the larger scale 1:25,000 Pathfinder maps. In either case it is advisable to protect the maps by laminating them or keeping them in a waterproof (and mudproof) mapholder, carried over the shoulder or fixed to the handlebars.

Route 1

5
Tower
Bredon Hill
Wood
4
N
3
Ruin
6
Fort
2
Lower
Westmancote
Overbury
Kemerton
Conderton
Beckford
Start/Finish
1
A435
Tewkesbury

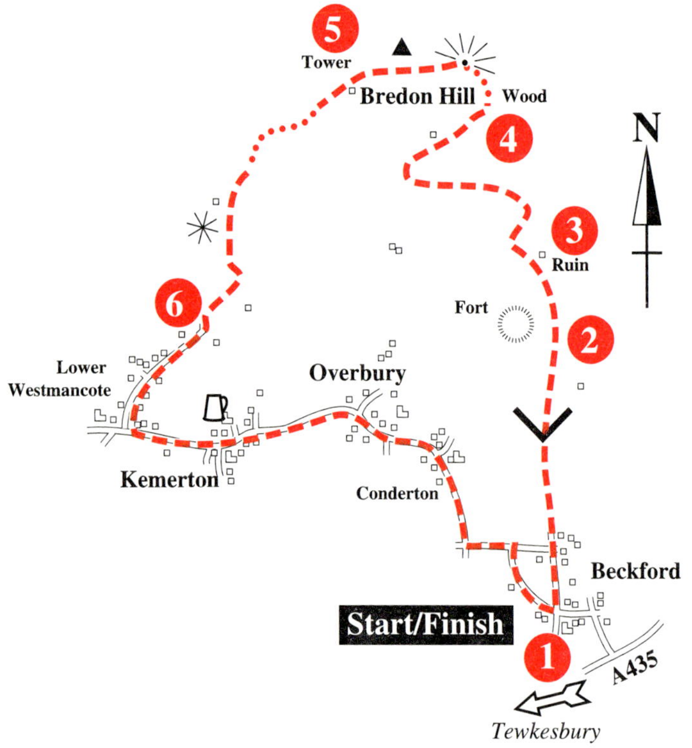

1

Bredon Hill, the Oolithic island north of the Cotswolds

> **Distance:** 10 miles.
> **Grade:** One strenuous climb, otherwise moderate.
> **Parking:** The car park near the surgery and tennis courts on the road out of Beckford towards Overbury. (6 miles northeast of Tewkesbury).
> **Start:** As above.
> **Height gain:** 860 ft.
> **Main climbs:** It is a climb almost all the way from the start to the tower. The first section to the end of the first wood is the steepest (600 ft.)
> **Maps:** OS Landranger 150.
> **Facilities:** Shop (open Sat AM) and PH in Beckford. Shop (open Sat/Sun) in Overbury. Pubs in Kemerton, Conderton.

Bredon Hill is detached by about 5 miles from the north of the main Cotswold range. This has distinct advantages in terms of views: you can see in ALL directions from the top rather than just the fine views to the west you normally associate with the Cotswold escarpment. Superb views over to Wales, the Vale of Evesham, the Severn and the Avon and of course, the Cotswolds. There are many different loops that you could devise on Bredon Hill: this one has been chosen for the tough challenge on the initial offroad climb, the fabulous views from the ridge at the top and the attractive villages at the base of the hill. Be prepared for sweat and lung burn on the first climb: it is unrelenting for 1½ miles and doesn't flatten out entirely until reaching the ridge by the tower at the top. It is definitely worth waiting for a day with excellent visibility before doing this ride, and probably taking a picnic to eat at the top, as it is a fairly short ride and you do not spend long on the ridge before the descent.

Places of interest

Bredon Hill Fort. Iron Age Fort with two ramparts. Site of a great battle in the early 1st century AD, the hacked remains of 50 men were found near the entrance.

Beckford. Silk factory and shop.

Kemerton. The Priory. Long herbaceous borders in colour groups. Stream and water garden. Open Thursday PM in the summer, some Sundays.

Overbury, Conderton. Scenic villages.

1. From the car park, go back towards Beckford. At x-rds after 100 yds, L on Court Farm Lane. At the farm, follow the track between buildings, then R just past a stone barn with green doors up a broad stony track. Steep climb to the edge of the wood. Follow blue arrows in the same direction through the wood.

2. At the end of the wood, LEAVE the broad, well-made track and turn L following the edge of the wood along the field edge. Go through gate and diagonally R uphill across the grassy field, heading for a point just to the right of the radio masts.

3. At a ruin, bear L on a more obvious track alongside the wall. Through gate and at T-j with main track, R. At 1st gate, L on broad track following line of fir trees. IGNORE 1st right turn on tarmac. Take next R at x-rds of tracks/tarmac.

4. With the farmhouse ahead, bear R through gate into field. At x-rds of tracks at edge of wood, L (maybe muddy). At end of wood, through gate and along LH field edge. At 2nd gate, SA towards tower following wall, then obvious track straight towards tower.

5. From the tower, follow the wall into the wood, on the main track. At the end of the wood, sharply L following signs, on grassy track down along LH field edge. At end of field L again on stony track. Follow this in same direction, ignoring left and right turns until reaching tarmac.

6. Ignore turnings to the right. At T-j with main road, L 'Kemerton, Beckford, Overbury' for 4 miles to return to the start.

Route 2

Kiftsgate Court
Hidcote Bartrim
Ilmington
Manor House
Nebsworth
Campden Tunnel
Ebrington
Chipping Campden
Start/Finish
Broad Campden
Paxford
Upper Ditchford Village (Site of)
Blockley
N

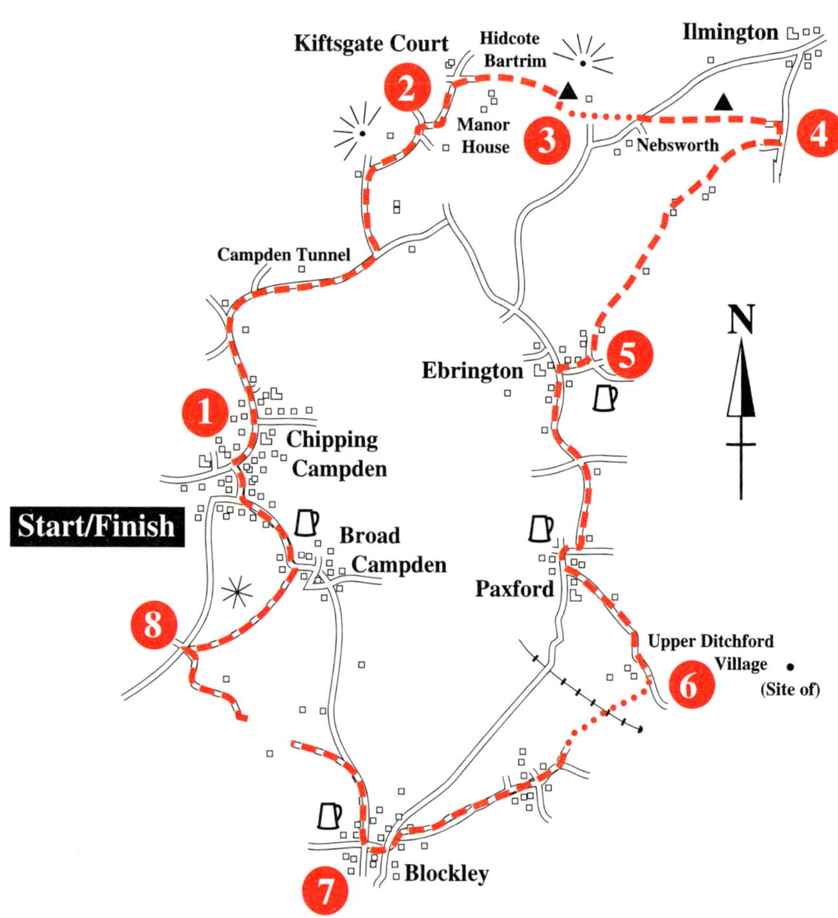

2

From Chipping Campden along the Northern edge of the Cotswolds

Distance: 17 miles.
Grade: Moderate.
Parking: Wherever you can. The streets are broad enough for parking on both sides. Chipping Campden is very busy with tourists in summer.
Start: Market Hall, Chipping Campden.
Height gain: 850 ft.
Main climbs: 330 ft on to the hill above Hidcote Bartrim, 400 ft from Blockley on to the hill above Broad Campden.
Maps: OS Landranger 151.
Facilities: Lots in Chipping Campden. Pub in Ebrington. Shop and pub in Paxford. Shop and pubs in Blockley. Pub in Broad Campden.

'Chipping' comes from the Old English *ceping* meaning 'market'. Chipping Campden is the last town at the northern end of the Cotswolds, the finishing point of the long distance footpath, the Cotswold Way, which starts in Bath. It exudes wealth and status from centuries past when its fortunes were made on the wool trade. The ride leaves Chipping Campden to the north and climbs to the top of the hills between Hidcote Bartrim and Nebsworth with fabulous views to the west and north over the Vale of Evesham. Descending past the lovely house at Foxcote, you pass through the attractive villages of Ebrington, Paxford and Blockley in the flatter middle section. A 2 mile climb to the B4081 sets you up for a fine descent into Broad Campden and return to the start.

Places of interest

Chipping Campden. The most important trading centre for wool in the Cotswolds in the 14th and 15th centuries. Market Hall – Jacobean building with pointed gables. Open daily. Church of St. James. A fine old 'Wool' church of Norman origin, restored in the 15th century. Woolstaplers Hall Museum – built in 1340 as a meeting place for fleece merchants.

Kiftsgate Court Gardens. Rare shrubs, plants and an exceptional collection of roses in a magnificent setting. Plants on sale. Tel: (0386) 438777.

Hidcote Manor Garden. National Trust property 'one of the most delightful gardens in England'. The Manor House is 17th century. The gardens were created in the first 50 years of this century. Tel: (0386) 438333.

Ebrington. Scenic village. 17th century manor.

Blockley. Well worth detour from main route. Used to boast six silk mills!

1. From the Market Hall, take the B4081 towards the church and Mickleton. After 1½ miles, by a small redbrick house, turn R 'Stratford, Mickleton, Hidcote'. 1st R 'Hidcote Boyce, Hidcote Bartrim'. After 1¼ miles, shortly after passing through small wood, 1st L 'Public Footpath. Unsuitable for motors.'

2. At road, L. (Fine views to the left of the Vale of Evesham). Opposite Kiftsgate Court Gardens, R 'Hidcote Gardens'. Where the tarmac ends, SA uphill on track. Follow towards masts, dog leg R then L near to the top.

3. At road, SA along field edge (may be rough). At corner of field, L down hill through trees. At bottom, cross field to a small gate in the far LH corner. At road, SA on to bridleway towards masts.

4. At road, R then after ¼ mile, R again on sharp LH bend. 'Foxcote House and Farm Only. Private Drive. Public Bridleway'. Bear R on main drive past Foxcote House. Past cottages, through farm buildings and gate into field. In corner of second field, follow the LH field edge down then up round two sides of the field to join better track past the barn.

5. At road, R 'Ebrington' then at village green in Ebrington (Ebrington Arms PH), turn L 'Paxford, Blockley'. At x-rds with B4035, SA 'Paxford, Blockley'. At T-j with B4479, R 'Paxford, Blockley'. After LH bend in road, 1st L then L again (both by triangles of grass). (Refreshments just off route in Paxford: Churchill Inn, shop).

6. Shortly after crossing stream and passing houses at the bottom of the hill, R on track. (Blue arrow set back from the road). At road, R through Draycott. At T-j with B4479, L 'Bourton-on-the-Hill, Moreton-in-Marsh'.

7. Shortly after the Great Western Arms PH, turn R 'Blockley Village Centre' then at T-j, L for shop/village (well worth a look) or R to continue route 'Broad Campden, Chipping Campden'. Down and up. Just before sharp RH bend, near the top of the hill, keep an eye out for a Public Bridleway sign on your left (a small track into the trees, sharply L back on yourself, easily missed). Follow track as it turns sharply R through scrubby woodland, then along LH field edge before joining better track. At x-rds of tracks in strip of woodland, SA.

8. On sharp LH bend, just before broad track joins road, R on track. Good descent with good views to the right. At road, L. At T-j with B4081, R to return to Chipping Campden. In main street, R to return to start.

Route 3

N
B4081
A44
Broadway Tower
Snowshill
Blockley
Start/Finish
Bourton Woods
A44
Moreton-in-Marsh
A424
Snowshill Hill
Bourton Downs
1
2
3
4
5

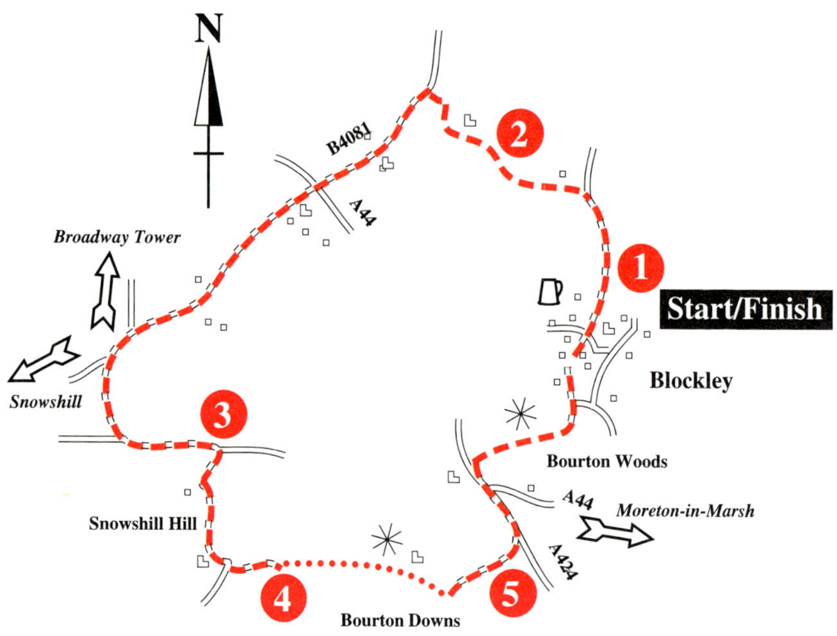

3

From Blockley over the High Cotswolds returning via Bourton Downs

Distance: 11 miles.
Grade: Moderate.
Parking: St. Georges Hall Community Centre, Park Road, Blockley (towards Broad Campden).
Start: The Post Office, Blockley, 4 miles northwest of Moreton-in-Marsh.
Height gain: 1000 ft.
Main climbs: From the stream, soon after Blockley, 600 ft over 5 miles.
Maps: OS Landranger 150 and 151 or Pathfinder 1043.
Facilities: 2 pubs and shops in Blockley. Pub in Snowshill, 1 mile off route.

This ride is largely on quiet lanes on the highest part of the Cotswolds with three linking offroad sections, leaving the best till last. Blockley is a charming little village, off the beaten track, most of it only discovered on the return into the village at the end of the ride. The route heads north from Blockley, dropping to a stream before climbing for almost 6 miles, offroad and on road to one of the highest points in the Cotswolds (316 mts – over 1000 ft!). If you want to see fine views it is worth diverting a mile north of the route to Broadway Tower Country Park. The cluster of buildings at Snowshill Hill has the feeling of a real estate community. A slightly rough section beyond Hornsleasow Farm through the woods near an old quarry leads on to a fine descent past lovely Bourton Hill House. A stiff climb sets you up for a very fine descent back through woodland into Blockley.

Places of interest

Blockley. The whole village was owned in medieval times by the bishops of Worcester. The small stream running through the village provided the power for six silk mills in the early 19th century which supplied ribbon manufacturers in Coventry. Many fine 17th and 18th century houses.

Snowshill. Just off the route but well worth a visit. One of the highest villages in the Cotswolds with superb views, a fine pub and the Tudor building of Snowshill Manor which was once owned by Catherine Parr, the last of Henry VIII's wives. The last owner, Charles Paget Wade, a true English eccentric, surrounded by vast wealth, nevertheless lived in extreme simplicity, sleeping in an adjoining cottage in a Tudor cupboard bed.

1. With back to the Post Office, turn L uphill, following signs for Broad Campden. A mile out of Blockley, having gone down and started up the other side of a hill, just before a sharp RH bend near the top of the hill, keep an eye out for a Public Bridleway sign on your left (a small track into the trees, sharply L back on yourself, easily missed). Follow track as it turns sharply R through scrubby woodland then along LH field edge before joining a better track, continuing in the same direction.

2. At x-rds of tracks in a strip of woodland, SA. Follow the broad track as it bends round to L then R and L again to the road. At road, L. At x-rds with the A44, SA 'Snowshill, Ford, Stanway'. Ignore left and right turnings for 2 miles until coming to a x-rds (with a conifer plantation to the left). Turn L 'Bourton-on-the-Hill, Snowshill Hill'.

3. After a mile, shortly after the end of the wood on the right, 1st R 'Snowshill Hill Farms only'. At buildings, fork L then turn L in front of house towards the clock tower. Just by the clocktower, R downhill. At the bottom of the hill, by a cattle grid, L on to track. Exit to road via white metal gate and turn L.

4. After ½ mile, as road turns left uphill, bear R on to track. 'Public bridleway' on stone marker. Shortly after entering the wood, L uphill on rutted track (blue arrow). You will probably need to push for some 300 yds in the same direction as the track broadens, at first grassy then with a stone base. Fine descent past a lovely farmhouse. Climb on tarmac to a minor lane. Turn L.

5. At x-rds with main road (A424) L. Shortly, join the A44, continue in the same direction for about 100 yds. Opposite the garage, turn R by a stone built lodge house on to track. Follow this beauty back into Blockley.

Map-reading on the Uley Bury, looking west towards Downham Hill

Route 4

Broadway
N
Buckland
B4632
Buckland Wood
7
2
Start/Finish
6
Stanton
Snowshill
1
Stanway
Lidcombe Wood
Stanway Ash Wood
4
B4632
3
Hailes
Stumps Cross
Hailes Abbey
Winchcombe
Farmcote
5

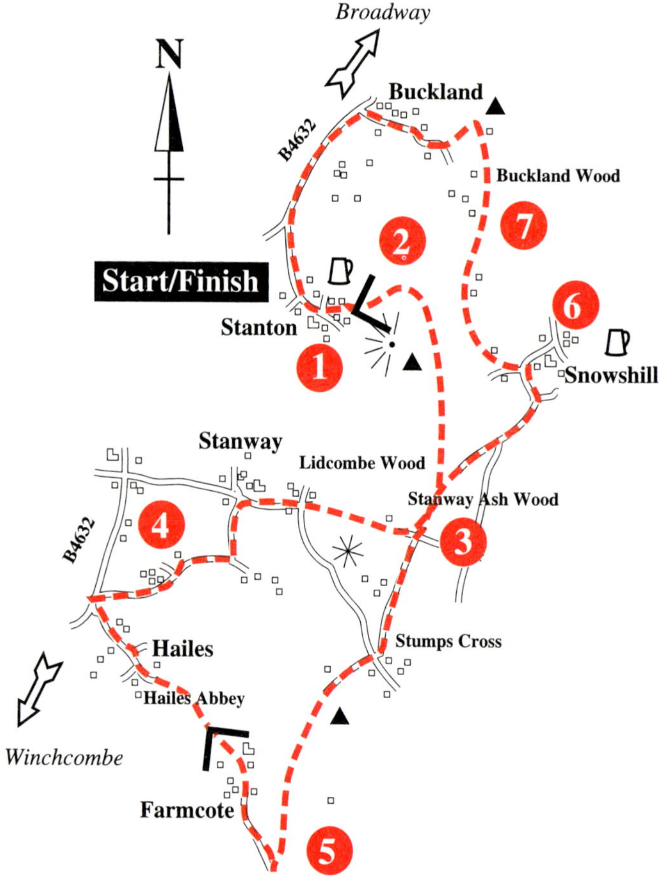

4

Stanton, Stanway and Snowshill. Steep challenges on the Cotswold edge

Distance: 17 miles.
Grade: Strenuous.
Parking: Small car park in Stanton.
Start: Stanton High Street.
Height gain: 1300 ft.
Main climbs: Two climbs of 650 ft – from Stanton and from Hailes Abbey.
Maps: OS Landranger 150.
Facilities: Pub in Stanton. Farm shop/tea shop near Hailes Abbey (open 7 days a week). Pub in Snowshill.

Two of the longest climbs and one of the best descents in the Cotswolds make this a real challenge for aficionados. The Cotswolds reach their highest point in their northwest corner. The escarpment also happens to be at its steepest at this point. The starting point, Stanton, is a picturesque village although you will have little time to appreciate this before an unforgiving 650 ft climb in just over a mile. Look behind you as the views open up, you won't have long on the top to savour them before one of those testing descents that shake you through and leave your legs on fire. Was it worth it? You bet! In a couple of miles, shortly after Hailes Abbey, you have to do it all again, although the gradient this time is easier and the ridge ride longer. There is a chance to peek at the pretty village of Snowshill before a more relaxed descent to Buckland and return to Stanton.

Stanton. Picturesque village, restored in the first quarter of this century.

Hailes Abbey. National Trust. Built in 1246 by Richard, Earl of Cornwall, brother of Henry III, having vowed that he would found a religious house if he survived the storm at sea that shipwrecked him off the Isles of Scilly. The abbey fell into disrepair following Henry VIII's dissolution of the monasteries.

Snowshill. Scenic village. Snowshill Manor – Tudor House. Fascinating collection of works of craftsmanship: toys, musical instruments, clocks, bicycles, Japanese armour.

Stanway House and Garden. Jacobean Manor House, Gatehouse and Tithe Barn.

Buckland. Attractive village. Rectory dates from the 15th century.

1. Up Stanton High Street 'Unsuitable for coaches'. Fork L towards Mount Inn, then just before the pub, fork R and take the narrow stony track starting at the back RH corner of the building 'Footpath'. This is an old county road, not a footpath so do not be deterred by the sign. The steepness will probably mean pushing for a few hundred yards but with any excuse, look back behind you as the views open up over the Vale of Evesham.

2. About a mile after leaving the pub, although it will seem much longer, at a x-rds of tracks with the Cotswold Way (signposted), go SA for 50 yds then next R through double green metal gates (blue arrow). Follow the blue arrows in the same direction, ignoring turnings and blue arrows to the right. After several gates, join a better track and continue to the road.

3. At road, R. After ½ mile, at 'Give Way' sign, where road comes in from the left, turn R on to track 'Public Bridleway' through gate and downhill. This is a magnificent descent (and should you be of a masochistic bent, a tremendous challenge to cycle up without getting off). In one piece? Join the road (B4077) on a sharp bend and bear R downhill. After ¾ mile, 1st L 'Wood Stanway, Didbrook'.

4. Follow signs for Hailes Abbey (you will go right past Hailes Abbey). At B4632, L then L again 'Hailes Abbey, Little Farmcote'. After ¾ mile, L on No Through Road 'Hailes Abbey'. You may want to stop for tea/grub from the Farm Shop / Tea Shop (open 7 days a week). To continue route, just before shop entrance, L on track 'Cotswold Way' (blue arrow). Steady climb on good surface, with views opening up. Past the houses at Farmcote on to tarmac.

5. Just before the junction with road by a triangle of grass, L on track into wood 'Public Bridleway'. Follow for 1¼ miles to the road. At B4077, SA '7.5 ton weight limit'. Carry on in same direction through 'Unsuitable for motors'. At T-j with next road, bear L, then 1st L 'Snowshill, Broadway'.

6. Shortly after 'Snowshill' sign at start of village, 1st L on No Through Road, (or SA for refreshments at Snowshill Arms PH and/or a look at this lovely village). After 150 yds, by triangle of grass, R.

7. Follow this track downhill for almost 3 miles, through the village of Buckland to the B4632. Turn L for 1¼ miles then L again 'Stanton' to return to start.

Route 5

Snowshill
Taddington
B4077
Ford
Pinnock Village
Kineton
Barton
Guiting Power
N
Wet Alternative
Cotswold Farm Park
Condicote
B4077
Ryknild Street Roman Road
B4068
Stow-on-the-Wold
Upper Slaughter
Start/Finish
5
6
7
8
9
4
3
2
1

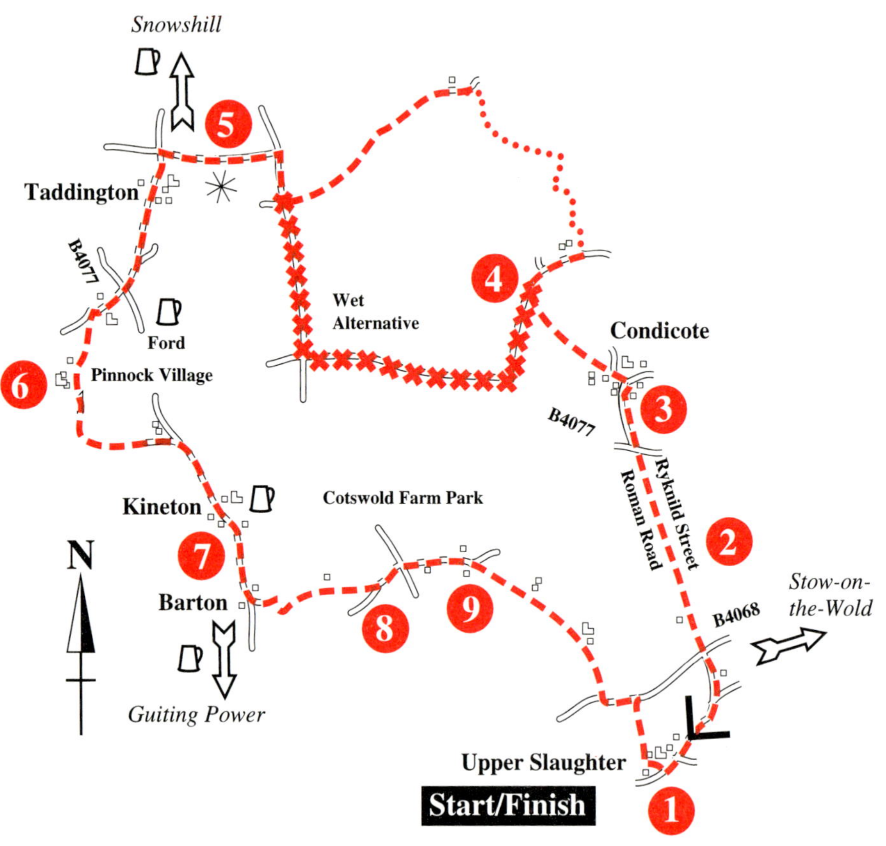

5

Upper Slaughter to Condicote and Taddington. The Northern Heights

Distance: 18 miles.
Grade: Moderate.
Parking: In the small square in Upper Slaughter.
Start: The Square, Upper Slaughter, near Bourton-on-the-Water.
Height gain: 950 ft.
Main climbs: 280 ft Upper Slaughter to high point on Ryknild Street, 300 ft from Condicote to Cutsdean Hill, stiff 200 ft climb from Barton.
Maps: OS Landranger 150, 151, 163 or Pathfinder 1043,1067.
Facilities: Pub in Kineton. Pubs just off the route at Snowshill, Ford and Guiting Power. Cotswold Farm Park (teas etc.) just off route.

Although not far from the busy tourist centres of Stow-on-the-Wold and Bourton-on-the-Water, this ride explores the hidden Cotswolds with few tourist facilities and even fewer coaches. A climb from Upper Slaughter (where you ARE likely to see tourists) takes you on to the old Roman Road of Ryknild Street which used to run from near Bourton-on-the-Water to near Sheffield. This route leaves you some way short of Sheffield. Maybe another day... Recent work on the drystone walls, the good surface and the fine views make this a most enjoyable section. Condicote is a hidden delight as is the dry valley north from Hinchwick where the birdsong echoing from the woods is a joy to hear. After a muddy woodland stretch and two miles on road, your spirits will soon rise with the descent to Taddington: fast, open, good surface, enjoy! A textbook bridleway after Pinnock Farm puts you on top of a hill for a fast road descent into Kineton. Except for two short road sections, good offroad tracks will take you all the way back to Upper Slaughter, with a particularly scenic stretch along the River Eye just north of Upper Slaughter.

Places of interest

Upper Slaughter. Scenic village, situated on the River Eye. The gabled manor house is one of the finest examples of Elizabethan domestic architecture in the Cotswolds. Old Post Office with beautiful kitchen garden.

Condicote. Scenic village.

Barton. Records show that by 1185 there were two fulling mills owned by those jolly crusaders, The Knights Templar, hence also Temple Guiting, two miles further north.

1. From the small square, L downhill past the Hotel. Cross the stream and climb the hill. At top of hill, 1st L 'Cheltenham 16'. At x-rds, SA on to track 'Unsuitable for motors'.

2. Follow this track (the old Roman road of Ryknild Street) over 2 more roads (x-rds) in the same direction 'Unsuitable for motors'. Note the fine work done on the dry stone walling. At 3rd road, (x-rds) SA on tarmac 'Condicote, Hinchwick'.

3. Into Condicote bearing L past stone cross and telephone box following signs for Hinchwick. At end of village, at fork of roads, bear L 'Unsuitable for motor vehicles' as far as T-j with tarmac.

4. Turn R (*) for ¾ mile. At the buildings towards the bottom of the hill, opposite a right turn to Condicote, L through metal gate 'Public Bridle-way'. After 150 yds, leave tarmac and bear R on to track around edge of wood. DO NOT go into wood but follow the track along the grassy valley bottom through several gates as indicated by blue arrows, changing sides to stay on grassy surface. Wonderful birdsong. Track becomes muddy in the wood and you may have to push for ½ mile. At road, bear L (in effect SA). After 2 miles, at x-rds, SA 'Unsuitable for motors'.

[*ALTERNATIVE route after rain/avoiding muddy woodland stretch: at T-j with tarmac, turn L then at x-rds with the B4077, R. At next x-rds, R for 2 miles. On a downhill section, at the edge of a wood, 2nd L 'Unsuitable for motors'].

5. Wonderful good visibility descent on fast track! At road, L 'Stow-on-the-Wold'. At x-rds, 1st R 'Ford 1½, Stow-on-the-Wold 7½'. At next x-rds, SA 'Farmcote'. Shortly after passing Slade Barn Farm (buildings on left and right), next L ' Pinnock Farm. Private Road.'

6. At white posts just before farm, L downhill. Good, well signposted track, although the final gate was locked. Follow track to road, turn L for a fast downhill then at T-j by New Barn Farm, R.

7. Through Kineton past the Halfway Inn on to Barton. Just after bridge on sharp RH bend, L uphill on track. At fork after 50 yds, R steeply uphill. At next fork, L (blue arrow).

8. At road, L. At x-rds, if you want refreshments, L for a mile, signposted 'Snowshill' to the farm you can see in the distance (Cotswold Farm Park). For continuation of the route, go SA at x-rds.

9. Go past gravel pits. Soon after entering wood, 1st R 'Eyford Hill Farm. Private Road.' (Blue arrow). Surface goes from tarmac to track to tarmac again. At road, L then after 400 yds, just before bridge at the bottom of the hill, R on 'Wardens Way' (Blue arrow). At T-j with road, R past telephone box to return to start.

Route 6

Winchcombe
Start/Finish
1
B4632
Sudeley Castle
Sudeley Lodge
Postlip
Hall
Short Cut
2
Corndean
Hall
9
Ford
8
Salt Way
Belas Knap
Long Barrow
Roel Gate
Highest point of Cotswolds
Wontley Farm
Brockhampton
7
Cheltenham
Whitehall Farm
5
3
6
Whittington
4
Syreford
Andoversford
N

6

South from Winchcombe, along the Salt Way and over Cleeve Common

Distance: 16 miles.
Grade: Moderate/strenuous.
Parking: Follow signs for Long Stay Car Park in Winchcombe.
Start: White Hart, Winchcombe.
Height gain: 1400 ft.
Main climbs: 700 ft from Winchcombe to the ridge road (the Salt Way) above Parks Farm. 430 ft from Syreford to Wontley Farm.
Maps: OS Landranger 163.
Facilities: Lots of choice in Winchcombe. Off the route: pub in Brockhampton, shop and pub in Andoversford.

Starting in Winchcombe this ride climbs steeply past Sudeley Lodge and Park Farm to a road known as Salt Way, which was used to transport salt from Droitwich to Lechlade, at the head of navigation on the Thames. Enjoy the views in both directions. A very fine descent drops you in Syreford, well refreshed for the next climb – an easier gradient but rougher surfaces. Deserted Wontley Farm has a post-Armageddon feel to it ; close to the highest point in the Cotswolds, it must have been cold in the winter – can you blame them for leaving? The descent after Corndean Farm to a ford is a tricky little number and the hills ahead almost look like Peak District moorland, very unlike the picturesque village image of the Cotswolds. By contrast, Postlip Hall is the quintessential Cotswold Manor House.

Places of interest

Winchcombe. One of the seats of the Kings of Mercia. Very prosperous in the Middle Ages due to the presence of the abbey founded by King Kenulf. The shrine of his martyred son, St. Kenelm, drew thousands of pilgrims and a great Benedictine Abbey was built here in the 13th Century, later to be destroyed in the Dissolution.

Sudeley Castle was in royal hands from the time of the king with the wacky nickname: Ethelred the Unready. It changed hands in the War of the Roses and again during the Civil War. It is now full of art treasures, armour, falcons, Catherine Parr's tomb, an Elizabethan garden and a restaurant.

Belas Knapp. Stone Age Burial Mound dating from about 2500 BC. One of the finest examples in the country.

Postlip Hall. Fine Jacobean Manor. Legend has it that whenever the statue of Sir William de Postlip hears the midnight chime, he comes down off the gable of the tithe barn for a drink at the nearby well.

1. From the White Hart PH, turn off the High Street down Castle Street. After a mile, as gradient steepens by farm buildings, R on No Through Road 'Sudeley Lodge, Parks Farm'. Contour to Sudeley Lodge, then climb steeply to Parks Farm, 'Wardens Way'. Turn L opposite Parks Farm on to a track by a triangle of grass and a second steep climb to road.

2. At road, turn R (this is the old Salt Way). Enjoy the views to the West. After a mile, at x-rds, SA. Take the next R after ¾ mile, 'Brockhampton, Andoversford'.

3. At T-j after 1 mile, SA on to track. Good fast descent on broad stony track to road. At road, R 'Brockhampton, Charlton Abbots, Seven-hampton'.

4. Follow the road into and through Whittington. Ignore right turn to Whalley Farm, take next R 'Cleeve Hill Common'.

5. At x-rds, R on No Through Rd. After 1 mile, at end of tarmac, bear R (in effect SA) on to rough track 'Bridle Road to Whitehall'. (First section may be muddy). Climb steeply through wood.

6. Exit wood via gate and continue along the RH edge of the field. By a metal gate on your right, turn L uphill along a line of telegraph poles. At tarmac, L passing Whitehall Farm on your right.

7. At gateposts with a large sign for Cleeve Common, go SA on main track. Go past the deserted buildings of Wontley Farm and SA onto a fast tarmac descent. Don't lose control as you need to take the first L (*) after ¾ mile sharply back on yourself towards a big house.

[* OR, for short cut/to avoid mud near ford, go SA downhill and R at T-j with B4632 and return to start].

8. Follow this lane gently downhill to a sharp LH bend by a wooden barn.

50

On the bend, go SA through gate (blue arrow, public bridleway). A stony, technical descent with good views if you can take your eyes off the trail. There is a muddy stretch near the ford.

9. Through the ford and up along the LH edge of the field. Exit via the first gate on your L and continue in the same direction towards a farm and the lovely old house of Postlip Lodge. At a junction of roads by a neat hedge, turn R and follow this down to the B4632. Turn R at main road to return to the start.

Route 7

N
Stone Frog
3
Kineton
Manor House
4
2
Roel Gate
Barton
River Windrush
Salt Way
1
Start/Finish
Naunton
Brockhampton
Wet
Alternative
Stow-on-the-Wold
Aylworth
5
A436
9
A436
Syreford
Hampen
Notgrove
Bourton-on-the-Water
6
7
A436
Salperton Park
8
Shipton

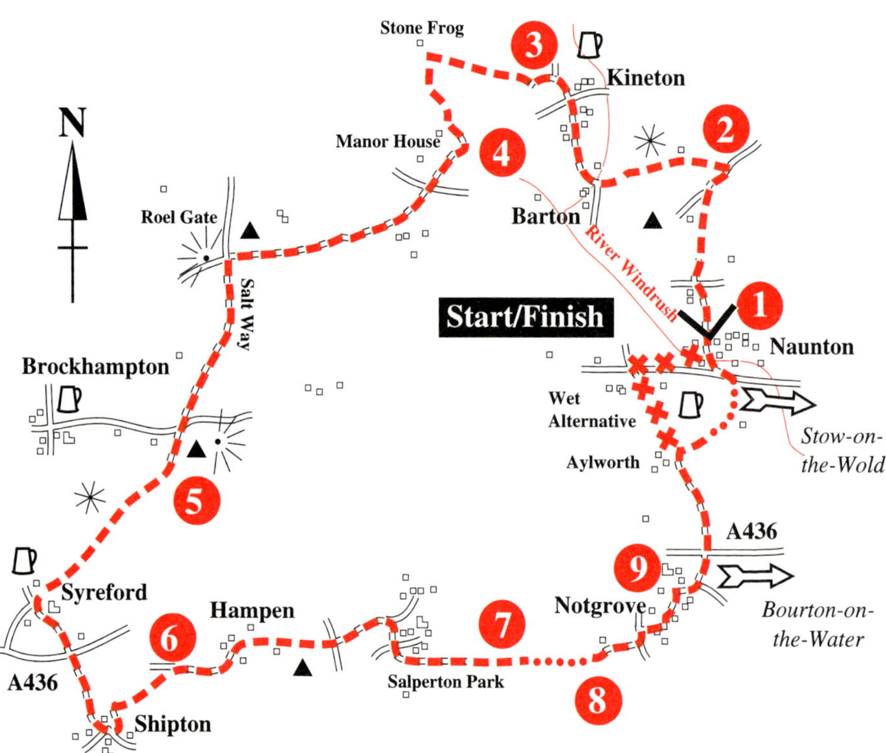

7

Naunton to hidden Cotswold hamlets

> **Distance:** 20 miles.
> **Grade:** Moderate.
> **Parking:** In Naunton. No specific car park. Wherever the road is wide there is normally somewhere to park without causing offence ie near the Post Office/ stores or by the church.
> **Start:** The Post Office, Naunton, 5 miles southwest of Stow-on-the-Wold
> **Height gain:** 1500 ft.
> **Main climbs:** 300 ft north from Naunton at the start, 300 ft from the stream in Guiting Wood to Roel Gate crossroads on the Salt Way. 270 ft from near Shipton to Salperton Park.
> **Maps:** OS Landranger 163.
> **Facilities:** Shop and pub in Naunton. Halfway House PH in Kineton. Shop and pub 1 mile off the route in Andoversford.

This ride is tucked away in the hidden heart of the Cotswolds. It links the hamlets of Barton, Kineton, Syreford, Shipton, Hampen, Salperton, Notgrove and Aylworth, none of which has achieved any cult status amongst the tourists, so be prepared for a pleasant surprise. The steep climb out of the Windrush valley in which Naunton is situated sets you up for a series of delights: the descent to Barton, the giant stone frog near Guiting Wood, the lovely lane alongside the stream in the wood, the views from near Roel Gate and the descent to Syreford. More tiny lanes, good tracks and little clusters of dwellings lead you to the ride's one 'field crossing' beyond Farhill Farm, east of Salperton Park. The field may be ploughed but it is relatively short, downhill and soon improves. Pass through the stylised little village of Notgrove, one last valley near Aylworth and Naunton lies beneath you in the Windrush valley.

Places of interest

Naunton. Scenic village spread out along the floor of the Windrush valley.

Guiting Wood. Handsome 17th century Manor House standing above its own miniature park.

Roel Gate. Crossroads 900 ft above sea level on the Salt Way. An Iron Age settlement at Grim's Hill lies ½ mile to the west.

Salperton. Lying on the Salt Way, its name is almost certainly derived from the Old English 'salt-paeth' 'Salt Path'.

Notgrove. There is a large monument near the church to the descendants of Dick Whittington.

1. With back to Post Office, R uphill. After ¼ mile, on sharp LH bend by Rock Cottage, bear R (in effect SA). Steep climb. At T-j, SA on to track. After 1 mile, at next T-j, R on tarmac for ¼ mile, down then up slight incline, then 1st L on track, sharply back on yourself.

2. Short climb then superb descent. Follow main track as it winds R then L down to the bridge. At the road, R over bridge. Follow road for 1 mile. In Kineton, at x-rds 200 yds past Halfway Inn, L 'Roel Gate, Charlton Abbots'.

3. After 200 yds, 1st R on track 'Unsuitable for motors'. Good quality track. At junction with road, by a large carved stone frog (!), L on grassy track past the frog. Becomes single track in the woods and crosses stream, At tarmac, L on delightful little lane.

4. At x-rds at top of hill, R. At white gate, SA. At x-rds, SA 'Roel Gate, Charlton Abbots'. At x-rds at Roel Gate, L 'Naunton'. After ¾ mile, 1st R 'Brockhampton, Andoversford'. Steep descent then steep climb: have the gears ready for it!

5. At T-j, SA on to track (or R for pub in Brockhampton, although it is a 300 ft descent). Fine descent: good surface, broad track, good visibility. At road, L 'Stow-on-the-Wold'. At x-rds with A436, SA 'Shipton'. In Shipton Oliffe, at 1st x-rds, L on No Through Road. Follow it as it turns to track by an electricity sub-station.

6. At road, R then after ½ mile, 1st L 'Hampen Manor' between lines of chestnut trees. At fork of tracks bear R, following tarmac track through farm buildings, down and up hill. Just past greenhouses, R on tarmac lane 'Unsuitable for motors'. This becomes a track by the last building.

7. At x-rds, SA 'Salperton ¾'. After ½ mile, 1st R 'Salperton Park'. Carry on in same direction through 'No Through Road' sign and follow tarmac to its end at Farhill Farm.

8. This bit may be tricky! Follow blue arrows directing you across field in

Typical Cotswold stone house

54

the same direction you have been travelling. The bridleway goes down the dip in the centre of the field towards a gate. (This may be very hard going in the depths of winter or after heavy rain). Through gate, turn R in grassy field and follow round to the L and on to better track past farm.

9. At T-j with road, opposite a pair of ornate gates, L then 1st R, 'Notgrove'. At a sort of x-rds, with the manor down a lane to the right, turn L. At T-j, R 'Cold Aston. Aston Blank. Bourton-on-the-Water.' Follow signs for Bourton to the A436.

10. At A436, SA 'Aylworth'. At bottom of hill, opposite Aylworth Farm on the left, turn R (*) on good track which soon deteriorates. Through double red metal gates with two handled fastener then bear L uphill on grassy track. Through similar gate and continue along RH field edge with new golf course on left. At road (B4068), R then after 200 yds, L on bridleway down along LH field edge. Cross stream and turn L to return to start.

[*ALTERNATIVE after wet weather. At bottom of hill, SA to x-rds with B4068, then diagonally R 'Naunton'].

Route 8

Start/Finish
Andoversford
Cheltenham
N
A436
A435
Withington
Withington Woods
Golf Course
Upper Coberley
Birdlip
Colesbourne
1
2
3
4
5
6
7
8
9
10
11
12
13
14
15
16
17
18

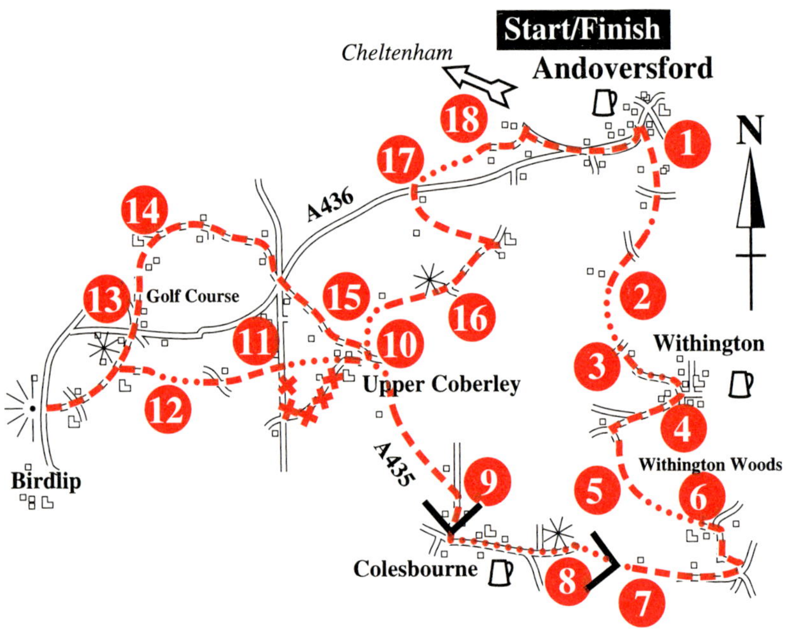

8

South from Andoversford to Colesbourne. Extra loop to Birdlip

Distance: 16 or 24 miles.
Grade: Strenuous, both for the amount of climbing and some rough sections.
Parking: On the broad street by the Victory Machinery Works, Andoversford.
Start: The Royal Oak, Andoversford, 5 miles East of Cheltenham
Height gain: 2100 ft.
Main climbs: 3 climbs of over 300 ft – after Withington, after Colesbourne and (on second loop) east from the A435 towards Birdlip.
Maps: OS Landranger 163.
Facilities: Shop and Pub in Andoversford. Pubs in Withington. Pub and garage shop in Colesbourne.

This ride has the feeling of passing through hidden, forgotten woodland and valleys which is surprising, given its proximity to Cheltenham. Although it lies behind the main Cotswold escarpment (you peer over it from Birdlip, should you choose to do the long route) it is nevertheless full of short climbs and fast descents, through woodland and in and out of many valleys. The second smaller loop is well worth doing (indeed could be done in its own right, starting from the car park north of Birdlip), particularly on a clear day, as the sudden opening up of panoramic views from Birdlip is one of the highpoints of the ride.

This is one of the toughest rides in the book and will become even more so in the winter or after prolonged rain as there are several stretches which will become muddy in these conditions. It is nevertheless one of the most rewarding, particularly on a day with good visibility.

Places of interest

Withington is a very pretty village well worth the ½ mile detour from the main route

Colesbourne Park is full of exotic trees brought back by Squire Henry Elwes (1846-1922), soldier, big-game hunter, botanist and forester. He roamed the world in search of exotic tree specimens. Hard life! Timber for the new bowsprit and masts of the restored SS Great Britain at Bristol has all come from the woodlands on the estate.

Birdlip marked the end of the climb up from the Severn Vale for the Ermin Way, a Roman Road that linked Gloucester (Glevum) with Cirencester (Corinium). The steep edge of the Cotwold escarpment is covered with beech woodland. Superb views on a clear day.

Seven Springs is the source of the River Churn, a tributary of the Thames.

1. With your back to the Royal Oak PH, L along the A436 then 1st L opposite the Primary School on to track 'Public Bridleway'. Follow in same direction between farm on left and barns on right. Cross a major road on to next bridleway, up a broad grassy track past farm to cross another road, over a cattle grid on to a tarmac drive.

2. Through the farm following the blue arrows. Beyond the farm, take the lower LH bridleway alongside the wire/wooden fence on your left. This track is at first bumpy and grassy but improves.

3. Go through next farm and blue metal gate following blue arrows. Keep to LH field edge and exit field via gate in LH corner. The track is once again grassy/bumpy. Follow this through several gates and over a broad track ('No right of way' signs to right and left) down to road in Withington.

4. If you wish to explore the pretty village of Withington or go to the Mill Inn, turn left. If you wish to continue the route, R uphill 'Hilcot, Colesbourne'. Steep climb, follow Colesbourne signs until reaching pylons and houses. Turn L on broad bridleway.

5. Go past a pheasant enclosure on your left. At the end of the enclosure, SA uphill on the middle of three tracks. In a clearing between woodland, follow RH field edge to a gate in the far RH corner. The next section may be rough/muddy.

6. At the end of a large clearing in the wood with tracks apparently going every which way, continue in same direction slightly uphill on less well-used track. Join the road just beyond the radio mast. Turn R then 1st R 'Woodlands Farm Only'.

7. As road swings right on to tree-lined drive towards farm, carry SA along RH field edge. In the next two fields follow the LH field edge, passing a small plantation on your right. At the exit of the enclosed track at the end of the plantation, keep to LH field edge and descend to a wooden field gate in amongst a small clump of trees. Go diagonally R across the next field to a metal gate at the edge of the wood.

8. You now face a hard, steep, muddy push. (It will be worth it, honest!). At T-j with main track, L to continue climbing along edge of wood then enjoy an excellent descent to road. Turn L, then at A435, R into Colesbourne (garage sells food). ½ mile past Colesbourne Inn, 1st R 'Hilcot'. Steep climb. Turn L on broad track as wood begins on left.

9. Follow this good track in the same direction, contouring then gradually climbing, ignoring a left fork through a field gate to a property. Continue to a lovely round-walled isolated cottage, turn L at T-j with major track and exit wood into field in same direction. At the road, L for 100 yds. If you wish to do just the short route, ignore the left turn, follow road round and turn R on bridleway (rough field edge) 'Wistley Hill' just beyond power lines carried by pylons. Rejoin at instruction no. 15.

10. For the full route, take the 1st L downhill beneath power lines. After the last building in Upper Coberley, R (*) through gate on grassy track in woodlands. The final stretch to the road is over an open field but it IS downhill!

[*ALTERNATIVE avoiding field. If the field beyond the woodland has recently been ploughed, stay on road, descend to A435, R then after ½ mile, by bus sign, L. Rejoin at instruction 11 '...bus sign...'].

11. At road, L then R just before bus sign down what looks like a private drive. It is in fact a class 5 road, number 50857 and you have every right to be here! Go round to the left of the house to continue in the same direction on a track. At road, SA for 100 yds then L through wooden gate 'Public Path'. Follow upper RH track at fork of tracks.

12. Head towards, then past masts on obvious track, through the subway under the A417. You should be rewarded with one of the best views in all the Cotswolds. Retrace your steps following signs for Rushwood Kennels until good tarmac track swings right towards kennels. At this point bear L (in effect SA) on rougher track towards wood on left. As this track swings right (the outward route), just after the end of the wall by the wood, bear L (in effect SA).

13. At x-rds with A436, (TAKE CARE!) SA 'National Star Centre, Ullenwood'. Just after the Golf Club, turn R on bridleway 'Leckhampton Hill. Cotswold Way'.

14. At road, R. After 1½ miles, at A435, diagonally R on to bridleway

'Cotswold Way' just by the 'Cirencester A435' sign. Climb steeply. At road, turn L.

15. After ½ mile, just before the pylons, L on bridleway 'Wistley Hill' along a rough field edge. At corner of field, go through field opening and follow along RH field edge of next field, staying on track as it veers right among trees to pass a great mass of pylons on your left. (From the road to the farmhouse is rough/muddy). Go past an isolated farmhouse (at present deserted) and follow the obvious track parallel to line of telegraph poles.

16. Superb descent to the road. Turn L and climb steeply for just over ½ mile. Where tracks join road from left and right, with the RH track going towards a farm, turn L 'Keepers Cottage'. Down and up passing a superb house on the left. Turn 1st R after this following the telegraph poles to the road.

17. At road, diagonally R on to very unpromising bridleway in field opposite. Go through gate turn R and follow hedgerow for 100 yds before heading diagonally L across field towards a gap at the RH edge of the woodland. Once through this, aim for gate then towards barns. Fine views left towards Cheltenham and the Malverns.

18. Through farm on to tarmac. At T-j with next road, L. At x-rds, R 'Withington, Cirencester' then at A436, L to return to start.

Wild flowers and woodland near Northleach

Route 9

N
Cold Aston
3
Cheltenham
Hazleton
5
4
Turkdean
Compton Abdale
A429
Fossway
Withington
A40
6
Farmington
Northleach
2
7
1
Yanworth
Start/Finish
A429
Chedworth

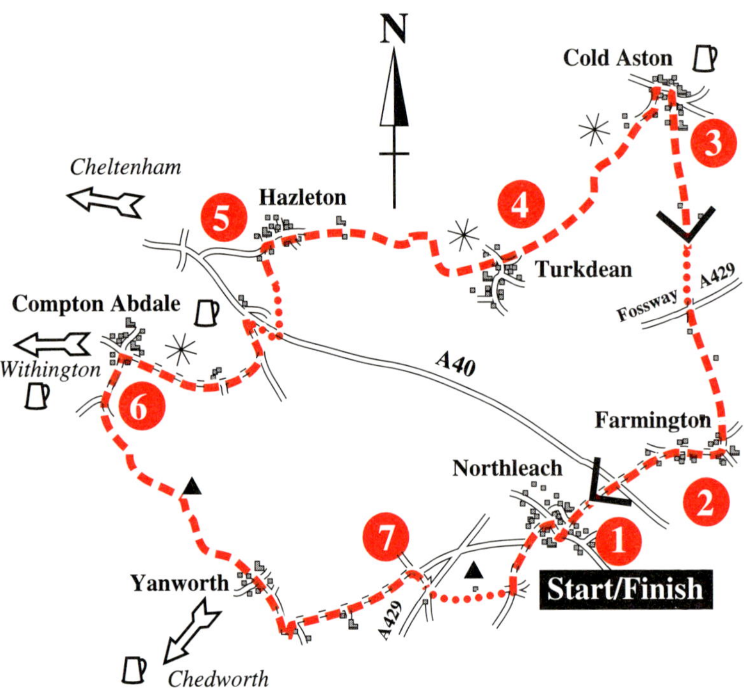

9

From Northleach to tiny villages in the heart of the Cotswolds

Distance: 17 miles.
Grade: Moderate.
Parking: In the centre of Northleach, no specific car park.
Start: The Red Lion PH in Northleach, just off the A40 west of Cheltenham.
Height gain: 1250 ft.
Main climbs: 200 ft before Cold Aston. 250 ft before Hazleton. 200 ft after Compton Abdale. 250 ft after Yanworth.
Maps: OS Landranger 163.
Facilities: Lots of choice in Northleach. Pub in Cold Aston. Puesdown Inn on A40 between Hazleton and Compton Abdale. Pubs 2½ miles off the route at Withington and Chedworth.

A string of pearls in the form of delightful little hamlets linked in the main by good all year round tracks. It starts at Northleach, up there alongside Stow-on-the-Wold, Bourton-on-the-Water, Bibury, Burford, Chipping Campden and Broadway in the 'Cotswold by Coach' category. No worries. You will leave that behind after a few turns of the pedals. North from Farmington, the council are letting this tiny lane fall into benign neglect — excellent news for mountain bikers! A rough descent drops you in a scenic dry valley before a climb to Cold Aston. The next section, to Hazleton, seems to be a favourite for many offroad cyclists, as you can depend on it being passable year round. Cross the A40, dive down into Compton Abdale, gawp at the picturesque water trough and wave a magic wand over your legs for the next climb. Yanworth's houses are all painted green, showing their allegiance to the Stowell Park Estate down the road. The final climb takes you over the Foss Way (A429), along a last stretch of offroad and down into Northleach.

Places of interest

Northleach. Scenic town. Surpassed only by Chipping Campden and Cirencester in importance during the Middle Ages as a wool trading centre. It used to be on the great coaching route between London, Oxford, Gloucester and South Wales. The church is one of the finest in the Cotswolds. The Museum, 'The Cotswold Countryside Collection' shows aspects of rural life.

Foss Way. (A429). Crossed twice, north and south of Northleach. Running for 182 miles between Lincoln and Exeter, the Foss Way represented the 'frontier' for the Romans between the softies in the southeast and the wild ragamuffins in the West and North. It is one of the most direct of Roman roads and it is claimed that it never diverges more than 6 miles from a straight line drawn between Axminster and Lincoln.

1. With your back to the Red Lion Pub turn L then 1st L along Farmington Road. Go under the A40 and at T-j, R towards Farmington.

2. At a triangle of grass in Farmington, L 'Bourton-on-the-Water' then immediately L again 'Unsuitable for motor vehicles'. Follow downhill to cross cattle grid then climb to the main road (A429). SA on to a bridleway (just to R of road sign) down a steep grassy track then diagonally R up the other side of the valley on obvious broad track.

3. Follow this track across several x-rds of tracks towards stone farmhouse and barns on the horizon. At tarmac, turn L. You are now in Cold Aston. At triangle of grass, turn L past The Plough Inn 'Notgrove, Cheltenham'. At the end of the village, just past the school on the right, turn L 'Unsuitable for motors'. This is an excellent track.

4. At a small cluster of houses (Turkdean), bear R at triangle of grass, turn R on the road then immediately L on track just past a farmyard with a large round grain silo. Descend and follow along the bottom of the valley. At a fork of tracks, with a red gate marked with a yellow arrow straight ahead, turn L through a grey gate towards a plantation. Emerge past farm on to tarmac and the hamlet of Hazleton.

5. At the end of the village, just before a large grey metal barn, L on a broad track. This track turns to grass before coming to a T-j with a track running parallel with the A40. Turn R on to this track as far as the A40 which you join near the Puesdown Inn. At A40, L then 1st R 'Compton Abdale 1½'. After 400 yds, R again. After a mile, swoop downhill. At Give Way sign, L uphill 'Yanworth'.

6. Steep climb. Near the top, just before a clump of coniferous trees, L through double green gates. At the end of this good, fast track you will come to the hamlet of Yanworth where almost all the houses are painted

64

Top grade RUPP (Road Used as Public Path) near Cold Aston

green, showing their connexion to the Stowell Park Estate down the road. SA downhill for 50 yds then at T-j, L downhill 'Northleach'. Down and steeply up, following signs for Northleach.

7. At the x-rds just past pylons, turn R 'Bibury, Cirencester'. At junction with the A429, SA through wicket gate 'Public Path' towards pylons. The track soon improves. At road, L to return to Northleach, following signs for town centre.

Route 10

Start/Finish
Bourton-on-the-Water
Little Rissington
Wet Alternative
Great Rissington
N
Cold Aston
A40
9
1
8
Clapton-on-the-Hill
River Windrush
2
3
7
Sherborne
Manor Farm
6
Great Barrington
4
5
Wet Alternative
Windrush
Little Barrington
Taynton
Burford

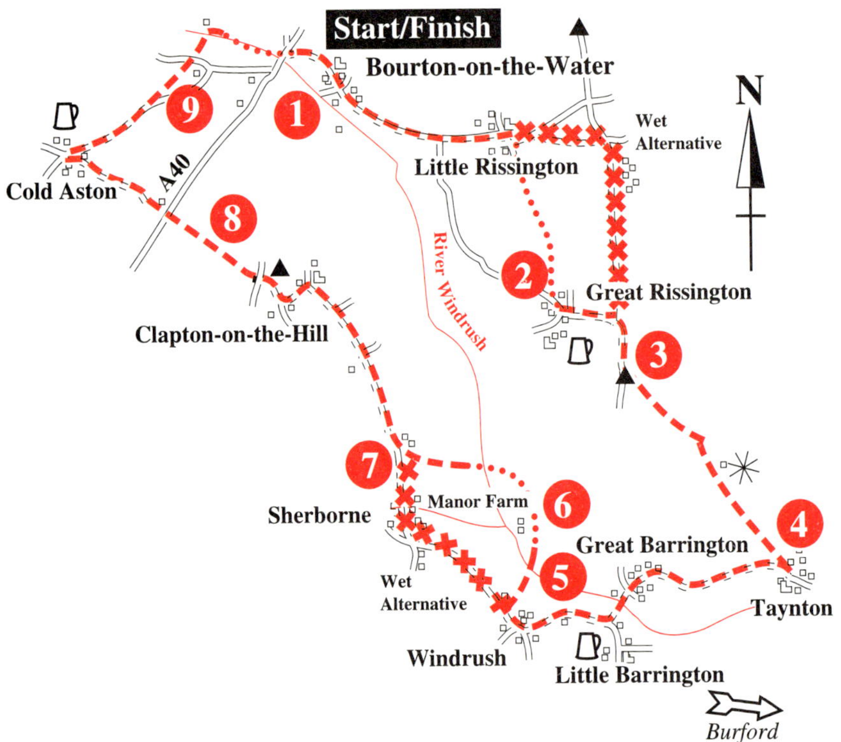

10

Bourton-on-the-Water to the Rissingtons and Barringtons

Distance: 19 miles.

Grade: Moderate.

Parking: Plenty of Pay and Display Car Parks in Bourton-on-the-Water. Be prepared to pay up to £3 for a day's parking. There is a large layby on the route 1 mile out of Bourton-on-the-Water towards Little Rissington with parking for several cars. If you start here, turn L towards Little Rissington and join instruction no. 1 at '...Little Rissington...'

Start: The Edinburgh Woollen Mill, near the Memorial Cross in the centre of Bourton.

Height gain: 850 ft.

Main climbs: From the River Windrush north of Windrush village to Clapton-on-the-Hill – 330 ft.

Maps: OS Landranger 163.

Facilities: Lots in Bourton-on-the-Water. Pubs in Great Rissington, Little Barrington, Cold Aston.

Bourton-on-the-Water is the Mecca of Cotswold coach tours so be prepared to see thousands of tourists. You will soon escape from all this so don't get downhearted. The route climbs out of the Windrush valley to Little Rissington to join a track heading south to Great Rissington. This can at times be rough, but better is to come. After another climb to a trig point on the Barrington road, a field is negotiated then you are rewarded with a fine descent to Taynton. Pass through the pretty villages of Great Barrington and Windrush in the Windrush valley. Ogle at the fine old buildings of the Manor Farm north of Windrush. Climb up to Clapton and Cold Aston before a return to base, partly along a dismantled railway.

NB. This ride is likely to be hard going (muddy) after rain or in the winter. Where possible, alternatives have been described. Marked (*).

Places of interest

Bourton-on-the-Water: the bird sanctuary at Birdland, the Model Village, the Cotswold Motor Museum and the Village Life Museum. There are many attractive buildings in Bourton but it cannot be stressed too much how busy the place gets at weekends and in the summer.

The Barringtons, the Rissingtons and Windrush are all pretty villages.

Windrush Church. Worth stopping to have a look at the grotesque beak heads around the Norman south doorway.

1. With back to Edinburgh Woollen Mill, L out of Bourton-on-the-Water. At T-j by Post Office, R. After 2 miles, in Little Rissington, after sharp RH then LH bend, on next bend by Manor Farm and Pound Lane, SA (*) on to track. The track deteriorates then improves. At bottom of hill after good descent, as track bears left uphill, LEAVE main track and continue SA along RH field edge.

[*ALTERNATIVE avoiding rough track between Little and Great Rissington. Follow road through Little Rissington, climb steeply. 100 yds after sharp LH bend with chevrons, take 1st R 'Unsuitable for motors'. At T-j with main road, R for 2 miles until reaching a white trig point on a RH bend by a lonesome chestnut tree. Rejoin route at instruction no.3 '...L on bridleway diagonally...'].

2. Follow blue arrows as the bridleway jinks R then L continuing in same direction towards farm buildings at Great Rissington. At road, L 'Barringtons, Burford'. Climb past Lamb Inn PH. At T-j, R 'Barringtons, Burford'.

3. After 1 mile, on RH bend by white trig point, L on bridleway diagonally across field (or in winter/after rain, do two sides of a triangle: from the road, turn L on track, at the end of the field, as track bears left, turn R towards remains of wall and clump of trees at RH corner of adjacent field). Follow track as it improves for long straight descent to road.

4. At road, R. In Great Barrington, at memorial cross, L 'Little Barrington, Windrush'. At Fox Inn, R 'Windrush, Sherborne'. Through Windrush past church and telephone box, following signs for Bourton-on-the-Water. At end of Windrush, just after the start of short climb, by a house with double wooden gates and an old style gas lamp, turn R (*) downhill on track.

[*ALTERNATIVE avoiding mud/soft ground near River Windrush. Do not turn R, follow road for 1 mile into Sherborne. On sharp LH bend, bear R (in effect SA) 'Clapton, Bourton-on-the-Water'. Follow this for 2½ miles. Rejoin route at instruction no. 7 '.. x-rds in Clapton-on-the-Hill'].

5. At house, L then L again to cross river. Follow the white arrows on the gates. Cross a large field towards double gates 100 yds to the left into the next field then diagonally R to metal gate over stream 'Please keep all dogs on lead'. Through strip of woodland on to uphill track.

6. At T-j with better, broader track, L towards farm (blue arrow). Lovely farm with old stone barns and dovecotes. Follow track as it winds R then L past buildings. Ignore tarmac lane to the right leading away from the farm, stay on track close to the perimeter wall. Continue in same direction to junction of tracks at a post with blue and yellow arrows. Turn L at post, cross river and continue on broad track to farm.

7. At T-j with road, opposite stone wall with ornate coping stones, R for 2 miles to x-rds at Clapton-on-the-Hill. Turn L 'Bourton on-the-Water 2¾'. Shortly, at T-j, R 'Bourton-on-the-Water 2, Stow-on-the Wold 6'. On sharp RH bend with road coming in from the left, SA 'Unsuitable for motors'. Take RH (uphill) track at fork.

8. Follow to road. TAKE CARE. Turn L then 1st R 'Cold Aston, Aston Blank, Notgrove'. At triangle of grass in Cold Aston by the Plough Inn PH, R 'Bourton-on-the-Water 2½, The Rissingtons'. Descend then climb TWICE. At the brow of second hill, opposite gate opening on the right, diagonally L on to track.

9. At road, SA (No Through Road). At bottom of hill, just after sharp LH bend, R on to track/lane 'Public Bridleway'. Through farm, however improbable this may seem. At next fork of tracks, R through wooden gate. Follow the bridleway through woodland and across field to main road. SA on to Lansdowne to return to start.

Route 11

Start/Finish
River Windrush
Windrush
A40
Windrush Camp
Circuit/air strip
Aldsworth
Ladbarrow Farm
Little Barrington
Wet
Alternative
/Short Cut
B4425
N
Burford
A40
Signet
Holwell
1
2
3
4
5
6
7

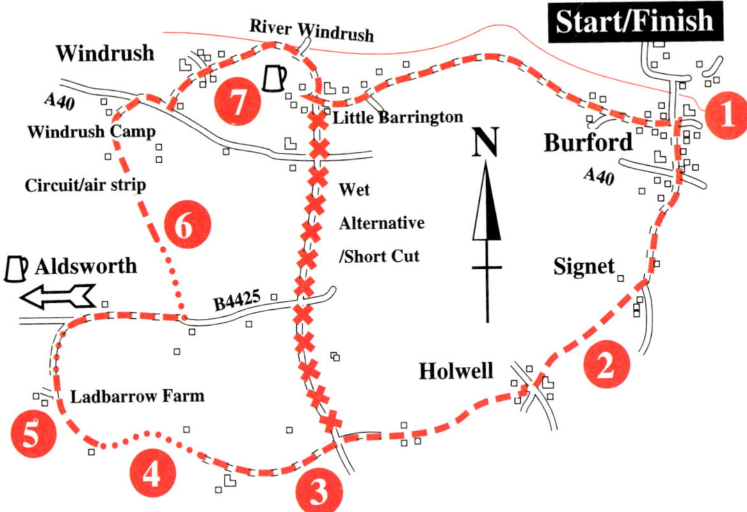

11

From Burford, over downland and back alongside the River Windrush

Distance: 15 miles.
Grade: Full route – easy/moderate. Shorter 10 mile route – easy.
Parking: In Burford, turn R at bottom of High St opposite Bear Court along Church Lane.
Start: The Tolsey Museum in the High Street, Burford.
Height gain: 200 ft.
Main climbs: None.
Maps: OS Landranger 163.
Facilities: Lots in Burford. Fox Inn near Little Barrington.

Burford is on the circuit for tourists 'doing' the Cotswolds. This might be perceived as bad (lots of people) or good (lots of fine buildings and places to eat and drink). Take your choice. The route starts a little unpromisingly, on the A361 heading south from Burford. But it IS downhill, and you are only on the main road for a short time before turning off on to a fine track that leads to Holwell and on to Holwell Downs Farm. Two short rough sections either side of the B4425 bring you to an extraordinary sign asking you to watch out for planes as you cross a grass runway. The last section, although on road, is wonderfully quiet and scenic, running along the valley of the River Windrush back to Burford.

Places of interest

Burford. Prosperity came to Burford in the Middle Ages through trade in wool and cloth and the great stone quarries at Upton, Taynton, Little Barrington and Windrush. Stone was used in the construction of Blenheim Palace and many buildings in Oxford. Burford's great coaching days date from the time of the turnpike roads and 'Burford bait', the huge meals served by the inns, was a byword among travellers. Many fine houses on and off the main street and a rural museum at the Tolsey.

Windrush. Grotesque beakheads around the south doorway of the church.

Windrush camp. Iron Age settlement.

1. Up High Street to roundabout with A40. SA on to A361 'Lechlade'. After 1 mile on this busy road (gently downhill), 1st signposted R 'Signet only'. Immediately R then L 'Right of Way. Holwell'.

2. Continue on this track in same direction. Where good stone surface ends, SA through gate along RH field edge. Into Holwell past church and memorial stone then 1st R on Public Bridleway (blue arrow on white circle) following telephone lines. At fork of tracks, L. Follow through farm to road. At road, L.

3. At x-rds, (*) SA 'Eastleach Turville 2½'. At next x-rds, just beyond power lines, R 'Public Path'. Follow past farm in the same directions as tarmac turns to stone track then earth track.

[*ALTERNATIVE after rain / avoiding rough stretch (shorter route: only 10 miles). At x-rds, R 'The Barringtons 3'. After a mile, at x-rds with B4425, SA 'The Barringtons, The Rissingtons'. At 3rd x-rds, with A40, SA (TAKE CARE) 'The Barringtons, The Rissingtons' then after ½ mile, 1st R by a telephone box. After 3 miles, at T-j, L on B4425 to return to Burford.]

4. Go through wooden gate at start of stone wall and continue in same direction through woodland. (Maybe rutted/overgrown). Follow as far as very wide gate with wheel (!). Turn L on good track. Through second gate with wheel. Turn R towards barn.

5. Just past a lovely farmhouse, on a LH bend by a clump of trees, R through white gate on to good broad stony track. At bottom of the dip through gate and the track becomes rougher/more overgrown. Follow to road, turn R and climb gently for 1 mile, passing two small lay-bys on the left. Opposite a farm lying to the right across a field, L on 'Public Path' across field.

6. Follow this across fields / race circuit / track / grass runway and between long, semi-circular metal barns. Just after farm house and before barns, turn R on broad track. At A40, R then 1st L by lorry park.

7. In Windrush, R past church 'Police Station', 'The Barringtons'. At T-j, R 'Little Barrington, Burford'. In Little Barrington, L just past telephone box. After 3 miles, at T-j, L on B4425 to return to Burford.

Old county road to the west of Duntisbourne Abbots

Route 12

Saltway Farm
10
Aldsworth
N
9
Saltway
7
B4425
Ablington
8
6
Start/Finish
Bibury
Akeman Street
2
5
1
Roman Road
River Coln
Cirencester
Coln St Aldwyns
3
Hatherop
4
Quenington

12

The valleys of the Rivers Coln and Leach, northeast from Bibury

Distance: 19 miles.
Grade: Easy.
Parking: If all the parking places in the main street are full, try by the church or buy a trout and use the car park by the Trout Farm!
Start: Swan Hotel, Bibury.
Height gain: 500 ft.
Main climbs: None.
Maps: Landranger no. 163.
Facilities: Shop, pubs, tea shops in Bibury. Pub in Coln St. Aldwyns. (Pub 1½ miles off route in Aldsworth).

Bibury is definitely on the Cotswold Tourist Trail. Set by the River Coln, it has many picturesque houses on or near the main street. You will pass many more fine old stone buildings on the ride, notably at Quenington, Coln St. Aldwyns and Hatherop on the outward section and in Ablington on the return. East from Hatherop you will spend a short while on the Old Roman Road of Akeman Street that ran from Cirencester to Aylesbury. The quiet, hidden valley of the River Leach south of Macaroni Downs Farm is an oasis of peacefulness and birdsong.

Places of interest

Bibury/Arlington. The Trout Farm. Arlington Mill Museum and Gallery. Arlington Row. All very picturesque, best visited on a weekday, or out of season.

Quenington. Lovely village. Circular dovecote at Quenington Court. Fine examples of Romanesque art above the doorways of the church.

Coln St. Aldwyns. Elizabethan Manor House.

Hatherop. Largely a 19th century estate village, the creation of Lord de Mauley, owner of Hatherop Castle.

Akeman Street. Roman road which used to run from Cirencester to St. Albans.

Salt Way. Used by pack animals to transport salt from the salt-producing town of Droitwich to the head of the navigable Thames near Lechlade.

Ablington. Fine 16th Century Manor House.

1. With back to the Swan Hotel, L on B4425 'Aldsworth, Burford'. After almost ½ mile, just past Hotel, R 'Quenington, Hatherop, Coln St. Andrews', then immediately R again down tarmac drive 'Public Bridleway'.

2. Pass amazing houses and a fine view of the hotel. Just past houses, ignore a footpath climbing steeply to the right, go SA on Public Bridleway. Steep climb through small wood to gate. Bear L at fork of tracks near gate past Xmas trees, then after 150 yds, follow main track as it swings uphill to the R.

3. Past farm buildings on rough track. Through gate and at T-j with another track, L downhill. This rough track improves as it climbs to the road.

4. At road, L. There is now a fairly long section on road, although all on quiet lanes. At x-rds, L 'Coln St. Andrews, Bibury' then at x-rds, 150 yds past the New Inn PH, R 'Hatherop, Lechlade'. At T-j in Hatherop by school, L 'Westwell, Burford'.

5. You will pass a lovely converted church on your left as the view of a small valley opens up to your left. At T-j, L 'Westwell, Burford', then immediately after bridge, L over the cattlegrid and on to the lane in the valley. 'Public path'. Over a second cattle grid. Where a small copse of trees almost touches the road on the right, fork L up a track 'Bridleway'.

6. At x-rds of tracks by a dilapidated barn, SA. Follow obvious track through black creosoted gates. At T-j with better track at the end of small copse, R. Follow past barn, ignore 1st track on left. On a sharp RH bend, with the large cluster of farmbuildings of Ladbarrow Farm 100 yds. ahead, L through a large white gate with a wheel on it. (Most of the gates on this farm seem to have this feature).

7. Just before the next farm (Dean Farm), R on to better, parallel track. Go past the farm, leaving all the buildings to your right, following the tarmac lane with the telegraph poles on your left. When the telegraph poles change sides from left to right, near a small copse of trees, by a fine house on your right, take the track diagonally R towards a wood. Follow the track

Bridge over the River Coln at Bibury

alongside the edge of the wood.

8. At road, SA 'Eastington, Northleach'. At next x-rds, SA 'Eastington, Northleach'. Just past a large farm with several round roofed barns on your right (Kilkenny Farm), L on track, 'Bridleway'.

9. Follow in the same direction, ignoring a right turn after 200 yds. ¼ mile after passing stone and metal barns on your right, at T-j with another track, R. There may be a short muddy stretch after a few hundred yards. At offset x-rds of tracks by more barns, L then R to continue in same direction. At the road, bear R. After 1 mile, having gone down to the bottom of hill and started climbing, turn L by Saltway Farm 'Public Path'.

10. At a barn, ignore a big yellow arrow pointing right, go SA past barn. Where you join a road, L on to track. Ignore left turn to new barn conversion. Follow stone / grass track to gate. SA along LH field edge. At T-j with road opposite a high stone wall, L. At T-j after ½ mile, R 'Bibury ¾' to return to start.

Route 13

N
A46
9
Painswick Beacon
A4173
Golf Course
2
1
10
7
8
Foston's Ash PH.
Sheepscombe
Edge
3
Haresfield Beacon
Painswick
Start/Finish
Slad
4
6
5
A46
Stroud

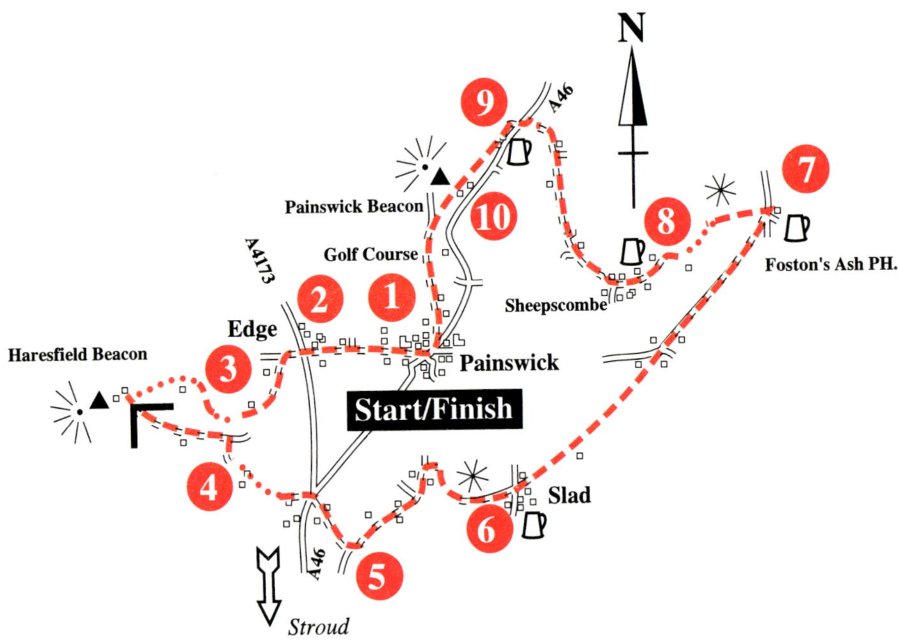

13

From beacon to beacon near Painswick

Distance: 18 miles.
Grade: Strenuous.
Parking: Car park in Painswick on the A46 south out of town.
Start: As above.
Height gain: 2500 ft.
Main climbs: It's all hilly! You can finally relax when you get to Painswick Beacon.
Maps: OS Landranger 162 and 163 or Pathfinder 1089 and 1113.
Facilities: Lots of choice in Painswick. Foston Ash pub on B4070 above Sheepscombe. Pub in Sheepscombe. King William pub on A46 before Painswick Beacon. Pubs just off the route at Whiteshill, Slad and Cranham.

This is probably the most strenuous ride in the book. This can never be said with certainty because wet and muddy conditions can make even the easiest ride hard going, but this one is bursting with hills, meaning lots of sweat, fine views and good descents. The topography of the Cotswolds around Painswick is fairly complicated: it lies on the escarpment edge and drops steeply to the west, hence the fine views from Haresfield and Painswick Beacons, but is also cut through by streams running down the Painswick and Slad valleys into the River Frome at Stroud creating more hills, descents and views. It is well worth waiting for a day with good visibility as the effort you will have to make to get to the highpoints deserves to be rewarded with views to savour. There are many highlights in this ride but alongside the views, the descent into Sheepscombe must rank high.

Places of interest

Painswick. As with so many Cotswold towns, Painswick's prosperity came through the wool trade and cloth production. The dyeing of cloth became a speciality owing to the purity of its streams and especially its spring water. Legend has it that only 99 yew trees will ever grow in the church-yard at any one time, the devil killing off the hundredth. The stocks at the back of the church were installed in the 19th century 'for the punishment of those who carry on carousels to the annoyance of neighbours'. So, however happy you are at finishing the ride, don't go singing about it!

Haresfield Beacon. A hill-top surrounded by the earthworks of an Iron Age promontory. Mighty fine views.

Sheepscombe. In the early 19th century there was no church here but eight unlicensed alehouses and the inhabitants had a reputation for drunkenness and riotous behaviour. The opening up of a Sunday School set them right!

1. From the car park, go uphill towards town taking 1st L on Edge Rd opposite the timbered lodge gate to the church yard. Down and up steeply. Bear R at the fork by the buildings in Edge.

2. At x-rds with A4173, SA 'Whiteshill, Randwick'. At 2nd x-rds after 100 yds, L 'Whiteshill, Randwick'. After another 100 yds, after row of cottages on your right, R on No Through Rd 'Stockend'. At fork of tracks, bear L uphill. Great views.

3. At T-j with road, R, downhill. Don't let yourself go completely! 1st track L 'Haresfield Beacon 1.5km, Cotswold Way' Some wooden steps. At T-j with road, by the farm, L very steeply uphill. Detour via the car park to the viewpoint for fine views into the Severn Vale and across into Wales. At T-j, R 'Whiteshill ¾, Randwick 1½'.

4. Just BEFORE a turning to the right to Randwick, L by letter box by Stoneridge Farm. Through gate into field, following edge of wood on your right as it bends away downhill to the left. Through a gateway down towards houses. Exit via gate on to tarmac. At x-rds SA. DESCEND WITH CARE to A46. R then 1st L 'Wick Street 1'.

5. At T-j, L, 'Bulls Cross, Sheepscombe'. By triangle of grass, follow road uphill round sharp RH bend 'Bulls Cross, Birdlip' and immediately R on stony track. Shortly, fork R. Climb steeply to top. At junction of tracks, SA and follow track to road.

6. At x-rds with B4070 by a memorial cross, SA. At T-j by house with old slates, L downhill. Follow to the end. At fork by sign 'Last turning point', bear L. Follow broad, main track gently uphill for 1½ miles to T-j by car breakers. Turn L, then at road, R for almost two miles.

7. 150 yds after Foston Ash PH, L on drive between two houses (the RH one is Ebworth House Farm). Go through two gates. Superb descent on main track, marked with blue arrows. After pond and a short climb, on a sweeping LH bend, bear L AWAY from main track which leads to black corrugated shed.

80

8. At x-rds, SA towards house. Descend to Butchers Arms PH. Past pub, 1st R after 200 yds 'Cranham'. Do not turn right or left, follow sign for Cheltenham towards A46. Just before A46 (you should hear it), L on gravel track with low wooden barrier. (It doesn't matter if you don't spot this: at T-j with A46, L).

9. At Royal William PH, R and follow tarmac to end. Where track forks, bear R past car park on obvious track then head for trig point. From trig point follow obvious track, bearing slightly R along wood edge.

10. At road, SA on bridleway on raised grass embankment into wood, following blue arrows. At road, L on to B4073 then at T-j with A46, R to return to start.

Route 14

Miserden
Woodmancote
The Camp
8
Througham
10
9
Lypiatt
7
A417
6
Start/Finish
11
Duntisbourne
Abbots
Bisley
1
5
Middle
Duntisbourne
Cirencester
Waterlane
Park Corner
N
3
Daneway
4
2
Sapperton
Stroud
Frampton Mansell

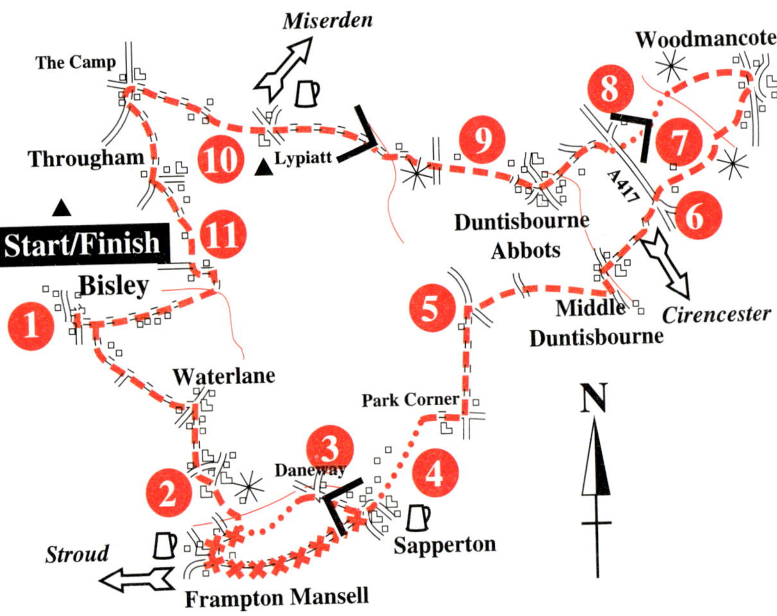

14

East from Bisley on bridleways and disused roads

Distance: 20 miles.
Grade: Strenuous.
Parking: No specific car park. Some parking near the Bear Inn, more on the verge on the road heading north out of Bisley past the Stirrup Cup PH towards The Camp.
Start: The Stirrup Cup PH, Bisley.
Height gain: 2000 ft.
Main climbs: From Sapperton onwards there are seven climbs of between 200 and 300 ft, as you cross one stream valley after the next.
Maps: OS Landranger 163, OR, Pathfinder 1113 covers 95% of the route (all except the easternmost section).
Facilities: Pubs and shop in Bisley. Pubs at Daneway, Sapperton and Miserden (the latter less than mile off the route).

A tough ride from the lovely village of Bisley with its two pubs, a tea house and village stores. The ride makes use of many roads which have fallen into disrepair and are no longer suitable for cars but are ideal for mountain bikes. The route crosses 3 stream valleys (twice), and the final one near Througham Slad just once. The ride is full of surprises from the Stroudwater Canal valley to the quiet Duntisbourne hamlets and the splendour of Woodmancote. Conveniently, there are road alternatives to almost every offroad section should you wish to do this ride after persistent rain or in the winter. They have not been described as there are too many of them: take a map and work them out for yourself as and when you need them.

Places of interest

Bisley. Situated at the head of the Toadsmoor Valley, this large village is a real delight with a 19th century lock up, many fine houses, wells and a couple of good pubs.

Thames and Severn Canal. Opened in 1789 to link the Stroudwater Canal at Stroud with the head of the navigable Thames at Inglesham near

Lechlade, it was never really a success. There were 44 locks between Stroud and the 2¼ mile tunnel at Sapperton and there were often water shortages at summit level. The last recorded journey was made in 1911 and it was finally abandoned in 1927.

Sapperton Tunnel. This was a 'legging' tunnel. The leggers were the men who had to propel the barges through the tunnel by lying along the sides of the decks and pushing with their feet on the tunnel walls.

Woodmancote. Scenic village.

1. With your back to the Stirrup Cup PH, take the upper RH road 'Waterlane 1¼, Eastcombe 1½'. At x-rds, 1st L 'Waterlane 1¼, Sapperton 3½'.After 2 miles, at x-rds in Waterlane at bottom of hill, R 'Oakridge Lynch ¾' then after 50 yds, diagonally L opposite garage with large double wooden doors 'Public Bridleway'. Good track.

2. At x-rds, SA 'Iles Green'. After ¼ mile, 1st R downhill 'Unsuitable for motors'. Cross bridge, DO NOT take towpath, but turn L (*) at T-j with broad track. At times muddy. Emerge at road near Daneway Inn.

[*ALTERNATIVE avoiding muddy section along valley bottom. Turn R at T-j and follow through woodland then up LH field edge to railway crossing. Cross with care. At road, L to top of hill at The Crown PH. At T-j by pub, L 'Cirencester, Sapperton'. After 2 miles at x-rds, SA 'Sapperton Village'. Rejoin at Instruction no. 3 …'Sapperton Village'…].

3. At road, R uphill. At x-rds 1st L 'Sapperton Village'. By church, take the bridleway just to the R of telephone box, through gate and diagonally R across field to bridle gate then on to more defined track.

4. Follow this through wood into large open grass pasture. Keep to RH side (may be bumpy). Soon join track which bears R uphill. Through farm at Park Corner to road. At road, L 'Duntisbourne Abbots, Winstone'.

5. After 1¼ miles, 30 yds. past black and white half-timbered lodge house, R through metal gate on to track 'Public bridleway'. At road, SA on to track. At next road, L then 1st R 'Ford'.

6. At T-j with A417, L then 1st R on tarmac track 'Public Bridleway'. At x-rds of tracks by farm, R towards track with grass growing in the middle.

7. Fine descent. On to tarmac drive. Follow uphill to road, turn L 'Raps-gate, Colesbourne' then 1st L by telephone box. Continue in same direction through No Through Road sign. Downhill to muddy section then steep climb to road.

8. At A417, R then 1st L 'Duntisbourne Leer'. At fork, bear L 'Duntisbourne Leer'. Through ford. 1st R 'Unsuitable for motors'. At T-j by telephone box, L uphill then at next T-j, L 'Duntisbourne Leer ¾, Daglingworth 2¾'.

9. Very shortly, at triangle of grass, R, 'Unsuitable for motor vehicles' then fork L on to stony track. At road, SA. At T-j of tracks, L then fork R downhill towards gate. At road, L, steeply uphill. At T-j, R 'Birdlip 4½, Cheltenham 10½' then 1st L down track by stone wall 'Public Path'.

10. Follow this steeply down then up on to tarmac to road. At T-j, L 'Bisley, Chalford'. 1st road L 'Througham'. On entering wood, 1st road L. Keep bearing R until road starts climbing. On sharp RH bend, by a wooden gate, L on to stony track.

11. At T-j with tarmac by large house, L downhill. At next large house, bear R on ascending track. At T-j with track by cattle grid, R uphill. At T-j with road, R 'Bisley'. At x-rds, R 'The Camp, Stroud' to return to Stirrup Cup PH.

Route 15

Stonehouse
Start/Finish
A419
Stroud
Ryeford
1
N
King's Stanley
Woodchester
Dismantled railway path
Stanley Wood
5
6
A46
B4066
Wet
Alternative
Nailsworth
Nympsfield
3
2
4

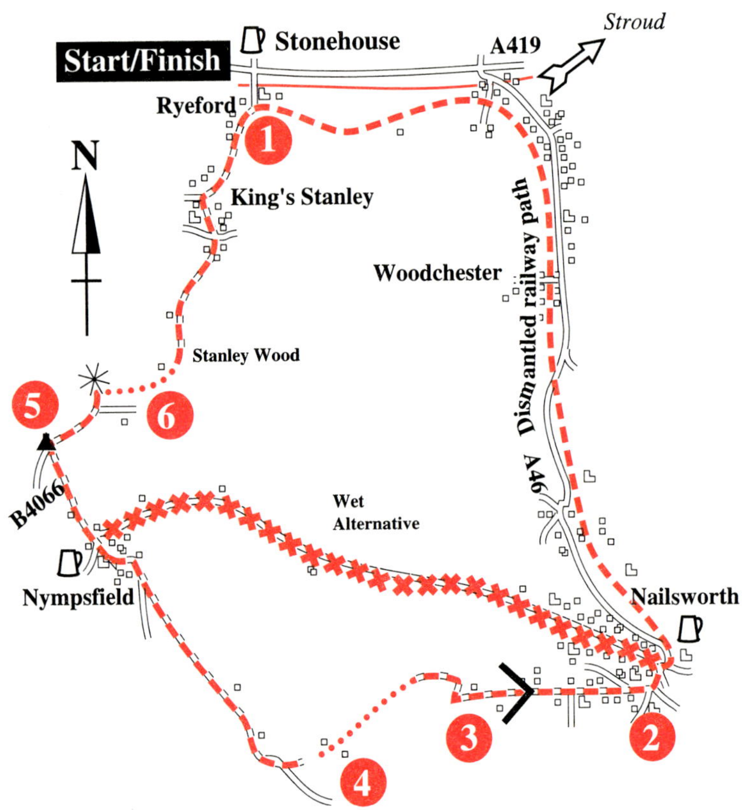

15

Stonehouse to Nailsworth on the Railway Path, returning via Nympsfield

Distance: 13 miles.
Grade: Moderate. (Easy if you opt for a 'there and back' ride on cycle path).
Start/Parking: Start of the cycle track at Ryeford, just off the A419 near Stonehouse. Follow signs for Kings Stanley then cycle signs. GR 814045.
Height gain: 630 ft.
Main climbs: Nailsworth to Nympsfield represents the whole height gain.
Map: OS Landranger 162.
Facilities: Lots in Nailsworth, pub in Nympsfield.

The Stonehouse to Dursley branch line was built in the 1860's and finally shut in 1966. Luckily it has been saved for recreational use: in the early 1980's the trail was built by the Stroud Job Creation Group. This cycle path, together with the Sharpness and Gloucester Canal towpath and the Cotswold Water Park near Cirencester, provide the best, flat, vehicle-free cycling in the area. Either side of the Stroud and Nailsworth valleys, the land rises to 700 ft within a mile of the valley floor, making for some fairly steep climbing by bike. The descent from Nympsfield is not for the faint-hearted, losing 500 ft in just over ½ mile down a woodland track.

Places of interest

Stroud. Built on steep slopes at the junction of five valleys, Stroud was industrialised around the start of the 19th century. It had established itself as the most important centre of the Cotswold cloth industry in the 15th century. At the height of its prosperity there were 150 cloth mills in the valleys around Stroud. There are now two.

Nailsworth. Another cloth town!

Nympsfield. Used to lie on the Gloucester to Bath coach road and there were five inns here. Gargoyles at the church.

1. From the Car Park at Ryeford, turn R on to cycle path away from pylons. Follow it for 5 miles, crossing roads as required until its end in Nailsworth near to the Railway Hotel. At the road, L on Bridge St. then R 'Nympsfield', then 1st L (*) on Old Market 'Town Centre'.

[*ALTERNATIVE to avoid mud after rain. DO NOT turn L on Old Market, go SA, following signs for Nympsfield for 3 miles. At x-rds in Nympsfield, R 'Selsley, Stroud' and rejoin at instruction no. 5 'At T-j with B4066.']

2. At the Britannia Inn, L on Old Horsley Rd 'Shortwood'. Follow signs for Shortwood and Wallow Green until fork in the road. Take the LH, upper road 'Wallow Green'.

3. 300 yds past the church on your right, as road veers sharply left uphill, turn R 'Lower Lutheridge'. Follow past the farm on your right towards the barns. The section near the barns may be muddy for a few hundred yards. Follow the track towards the wood. Through gate into field and follow RH field edge. At next gate aim for telegraph pole at end of field.

4. Follow the upper, LH track (blue arrows), leaving the farm below you to your right. Join tarmac just past farm and turn L. Follow this lane, bearing right, following signs for Nympsfield. In Nympsfield, go past the Rose and Crown PH. At x-rds, SA 'Selsley 4, Stroud 6'.

5. At T-j with B4066, R 'Stroud 5'. DO NOT take 1st Bridleway on left, but the second on L, 200 yds past the Bus Stop, just after a 'Bend in road' sign. (Keep a sharp eye out for this instruction). The first part may be muddy. At x-rds of tracks, SA downhill.

6. Steep downhill, at times technical and muddy. Join tarmac. At small roundabout, SA. At T-j by shops, bear R 'Selsley, Stroud'. After a mile, opposite small electricity sub station, R to return to car park at start of cycle track.

Route 16

Start/Finish
A38
M5
Tilsdown
Cam
2
3
Stinchcombe Hill
supermarket
Dursley
A4135
4
1
Cam Long Down
10
9
Uley Bury
Downham Hill
Uley
8
6
7
Folly Wood
W o o d l a n d
5
Stroud
B4066
N

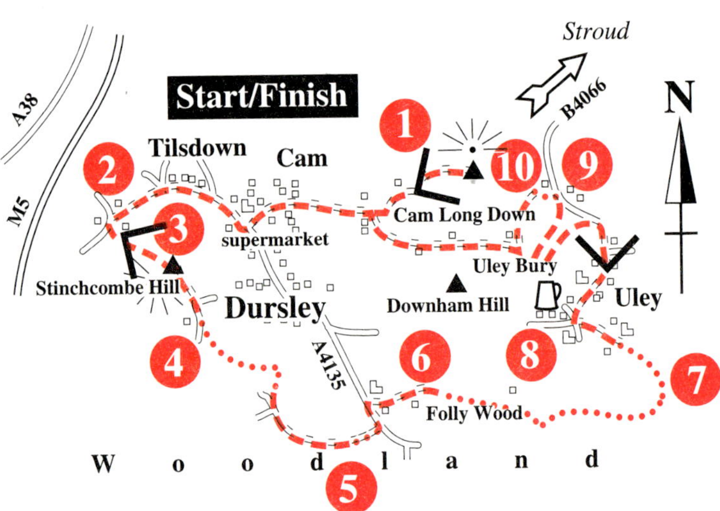

16

Steep wooded hills around Dursley. Uley Bury. Cam Long Down

Distance: 13 miles.
Grade: Strenuous (both for the hard going in the woods and the hills).
Parking: Cam Long Down Car Park, northeast of Dursley. GR 767994.
To get to the car park from Dursley, take the A4135 northwest towards the M5. Just before Quik Save on the left, turn right on Kingshill Lane, signposted 'Upper Cam, Coaley, St. Georges Church'. After ¾ mile, just after telephone box and bus stop on the right, turn right on Springhill for a further ¾ mile. The Car Park beneath Cam Long Down is on your right.
Start: As above.
Height gain: 1500 ft. (1050 without Uley Bury). Cam Long Down – 330 ft.
Main climbs: Stinchcombe Hill – 330 ft. East from Dursley, in the woods, 330 ft. Uley to Uley Bury – 450 ft. Cam Long Down – 330 ft.
Maps: Best is OS Pathfinder 1132. Otherwise, OS Landranger 162.
Facilities: Lots of choice in Dursley. Pub and shop in Uley.

This is a short, tough ride with some magnificent views at several points along the route and maybe some encounters with the dreaded Cotswold mud. Best avoided in the depths of winter or after prolonged rain, as the wooded sections can get very nasty! Wear appropriate footwear. Gloucestershire County Council are aware of the mud problem but if you want to add your voice, write to the Rights of Way Department in Gloucester (address in Introduction). The ride gets most of the road section out of the way at the beginning, giving you a chance to warm up before the first severe test: the climb up Stinchcombe Hill. Bet you can't make it to the top without getting off! This is very abrupt but the woods are lovely and the views from the golf course at the top are fabulous. Apart from a short stretch in the open on the A4135, you are on woodland tracks for the next 4 miles. Just before joining the road into Uley you will come across some amazing tree roots that look as though they belong in Lord of the Rings. Another steep climb up Crawley Hill takes you to the old Iron Age hill fort of Uley Bury with more good views over to the odd shapes of Downham Hill, Peaked Down and Cam Long Down. Rattle your way downhill and take quiet lanes back to the Car Park. If you have any energy left, a side trip on to Cam Long Down offers the day's best views.

Places of interest

Dursley. Busy market town centred on the delightful 18th century market house, which is also the Town Hall. Church has a fine perpendicular porch and Gothic tower.

Uley. Many fine 18th century houses.

Uley Bury. Most commanding Iron Age fort in the Cotswolds covering a massive 32 acres. Fine views in every direction.

Cam Long Down. Oolithic humpback. Superb views.

1. From car park, L for a mile. At T-j at the end of Springhill, L on Church Road. At T-j with Kingshill Road (A4135), R 'Gloucester 14, Wotton 6' then opposite Magistrate Court, L 'Sharpness.'

2. On sharp RH bend, L 'Stinchcombe, Wotton'. After 600 yds. at start of village, keep your eye out for a track on the L 'Public Bridleway. Stinchcombe Hill 0.5 km'. Steep, lovely wooded climb.

3. At top, follow track, crossing golf fairways with care, following in the same direction to join tarmac track near 4th tee. Bear R towards the club house. 100 yds. past club house, L downhill opposite tall stone wall 'Dursley' then immediately R on Public Bridleway staying on upper track.

4. Follow upper track (blue arrows). The first few hundred yards may be muddy in sections. Avoid losing height, contouring until joining road opposite stone wall. Turn L for ½ mile. Go past Nuclear Electric compound on your right. IGNORE 1st Public Bridleway on left, opposite 1st farm track on the right. Opposite 2nd farm track on your right, at a post on your left with TWO bridleway signs, bear L on the bridleway between wooden posts that starts off parallel with road.

5. Stay on upper track (you will have to lift your bike over wooden barriers) until reaching the road at an escape route. Turn L (*) downhill. Just past 'Dursley' sign, before 30 mph signs, R on bridleway 'Uley'. At three way split of tracks, take RH track.

[* ALTERNATIVE to avoid mud in wood. Turn R uphill. Follow the main road (A4135) for 2 miles. 1st L on B4058 'Nailsworth' then after ¼ mile, L again 'Uley'. Rejoin route at instruction no. 8 'At x-rds...'].

6. With metal gate ahead, bear R on track towards woodland. Stay on lower track until x-rds of tracks. At this point go SA on slightly rising track. Go past house with an amazing rusty collection of old trucks and tractors. Just past house, fork R uphill. The next mile and a half is either steep or muddy or both! At T-j at top of climb, L downhill. Follow the track closest to the lower edge of the wood. If you are in thick mud, remember to write to Gloucester County Council.

7. Giving instructions in any wood are difficult, in this one particularly so. Keep an eye out for the first left downhill in a clearing, which will take you past some fine hobgoblinesque tree roots. Exit field via gate on to road. Turn L towards Uley. (If you miss the left turn, do not worry, you will emerge on the road slightly higher up. Turn L downhill).

8. At x-rds, R 'Stroud 7½, Gloucester 15½'. Go through Uley. Steep climb up Crawley Hill. At a layby at the top of the steep section of the hill with fine views northwest over the Severn Vale, sharply L back on yourself.

9. Bear L at fork of tracks through wooden height barrier into small car park. Complete a circuit of Uley Bury without losing height. Return to point where the bridleway joins the road. Do not go on to road, instead turn L downhill then sharply L again, steeply downhill on the Cotswold Way. Muddy section at the bottom.

10. Join farm track, continue to road. At road, bear L, then after ¼ mile, 1st R 'Cam'. At T-j at end of Farfield, R 'Cam, Coaley' then after 200 yds, at T-j at the end of Drake Lane, R 'Ashmead, Coaley' to return to Car Park.

Side trip on to Cam Long Down

From Car Park, take track uphill towards house with grey slate roof then bear L uphill on to sunken gravel track. At x-rds of tracks, L uphill to top of ridge for magnificent views of the Severn Vale and lots of the Cotswolds. This is unfortunately a 'there and back again' side trip as the bridleway mysteriously turns into a footpath at the end of the ridge.

Route 17

Stroud
Start/Finish
Nailsworth
Box
1
2
Minchinhampton
Hard route (b)
A46
Easy route (a)
8
Avening
7
6
N
Daneway
Course of old canal
4
5
Sapperton
Frampton Mansell
A419
A419
Cirence.
Disused Airfield
3

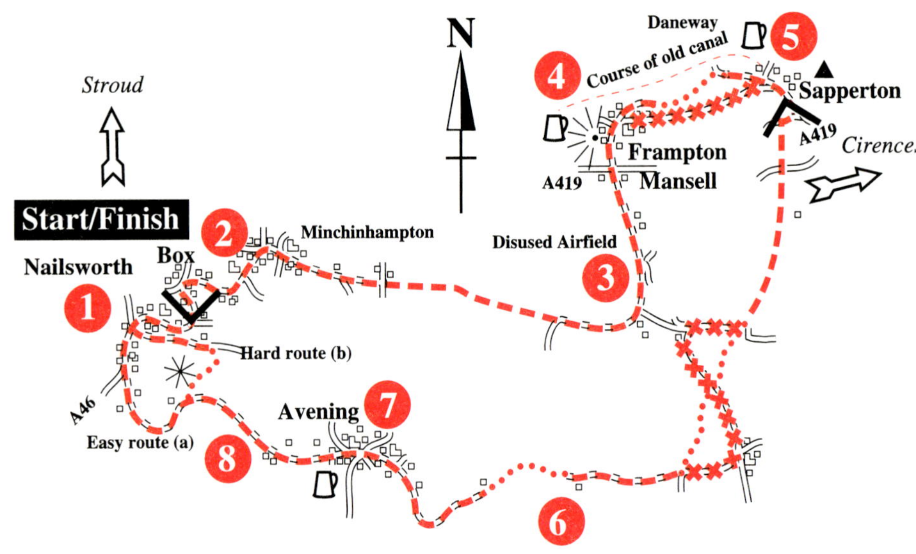

17

From Nailsworth to Sapperton via Minchinhampton and the Frome valley

Distance: 19 miles.
Grade: Moderate/strenuous.
Parking: Free Car Park near Britannia Inn along Old Market in centre of Nailsworth.
Start: Clocktower, Nailsworth.
Height gain: 1100 ft.
Main climbs: 430 ft from Nailsworth up to Minchinhampton. Sharp 200 ft from Daneway to above Sapperton, 200 ft from Avening to the wood above Nailsworth.
Maps: OS Landranger 162 and 163 or Pathfinders 1113 and 1133.
Facilities: Shops and pubs in Nailsworth, Minchinhampton, Avening. Pubs in Frampton Mansell and Sapperton.

Nailsworth and nearby Stroud represent the industrial past of the Cotswolds. Both are set in steep valleys which contain the streams that used to drive the mills when the wool trade flourished. The ride begins with a fairly long road climb (4 miles) on quiet lanes out of the Nailsworth valley via the delightful villages of Box and Minchinhampton. From here the route heads east, passing a disused airfield then the lovely Italianate Church in Frampton Mansell, with splendid views over the Frome Valley. Cross the railway line with extreme care and drop to the valley floor, following the river/disused Thames and Severn Canal along an old county road. The Daneway pub makes a good refreshment stop but don't forget the hill to Sapperton! More old county roads, cutting across the existing network and deteriorating as they go south lead on to Avening. Another climb affords wide views across the Nailsworth Valley to Minchinhampton Common. Swoop down the final descent back to the start.

Places of interest

Minchinhampton. Became prosperous with the production of cloth. Late 17th century Market House, the Post Office is Queen Anne. The Church has many interesting features including some monumental brasses.

Thames and Severn Canal. Designed to link the Stroudwater canal with the navigable Thames at Lechlade, it was never a great success because of the number of locks between Stroud and the 2¼ mile tunnel starting in Sapperton and problems in maintaining water levels on the upper stretches.

Frampton Mansell. Handsome neo-Norman church. Fine views.

Avening. Prosperous from cloth manufacture. There is an effigy in the church of the pirate son of Lord Chandos of Sudeley, Henry Bridges who in his youth 'indulged in deeds of lawlessness and robbery almost unsurpassed'.

1. From Clocktower, take George Street for 300 yds. 1st R after cattle grid on Pensile Road. After ¾ mile, at fork, L uphill '6 ft 6'. At x-rds at the top of Scar Hill, R 'Box'. At next x-rds by house called Waysmeet, R.

2. At T-j at the end of Box Lane, R. After 200 yds, at second T-j, L. At 3rd T-j, with a row of stone terraced houses ahead, R on West End. Follow through Minchinhampton as it becomes Tetbury Street. After cattle grid, fork 1st L on to minor road by a holly tree. At x-rds, SA. Follow this track past airfield to road. At road, L.

3. At x-rds, L 'Frampton Mansell 1½'. At x-rds with A419, SA 'Frampton Mansell ½'. Into Frampton Mansell. At The Crown PH (*), L downhill 'Unsuitable for long vehicles'. After 200 yds, on sharp LH bend by triangle of grass, R 'Unsuitable for motor vehicles'.

[* ALTERNATIVE avoiding the valley track to Sapperton which may be muddy after rain. Go SA at The Crown PH 'Sapperton'. After 2 miles, at x-rds, turn R and rejoin route at instruction no. 5 '...At 2nd x-rds, R....'].

4. WITH EXTREME CARE, cross railway line, shutting both gates. Follow track downhill along RH field edge, through gate, bearing R at T-j of tracks by 3 small thorn bushes and along the valley for 1½ miles. At T-j where the track joins the road, turn R uphill (or L for The Daneway Inn).

5. At 1st x-rds, SA 'Cirencester, Kemble'. At 2nd x-rds, R 'Cherington 4, Stroud 7½'. After 200 yds, 1st L on track. At 1st road, R then L on to track. At 2nd road (*), L then R 'Public Path'. This may be rutted/bumpy. At 3rd road, SA. This may also be in poor state. At road R, then R again immediately at T-j, 'Cherington'.

[* ROAD ALTERNATIVE – at 2nd road, R. At T-j after ¾ mile, L 'Rodmarton 1½'. At x-rds in Rodmarton, R 'Cherington'. At T-j after 1 mile, R 'Cherington'. Rejoin at start of instruction no. 6].

6. At T-j with 'Cherington' to the right and 'Culkerton' to the left, go SA on to Public Bridleway. (Rough track). At road by electricity sub-station, SA 'Avening 1½'. Just before the next T-j, R on track.

7. At road, L on tarmac. At x-rds with larger road, L again. After 100 yds, at T-j with B4014, R 'Nailsworth'. After 200 yds, by the telephone box, L on Point Road. Ignore Pound Hill on left. Shortly, at T-j, L and follow this on to 'West End. No Through Road' and past sign for Orchard House.

8. Tarmac turns to track. Enter wood. After ½ mile in wood, on a LH bend with a ruined stone barn and two metal gates to your right, you choose:
a) Easy. Go SA. After ½ mile, just after track to the left signposted with a yellow arrow, 1st R at fork of tracks. Follow downhill as it becomes tarmac. At A46, R down into Nailsworth back to the start.
b) Hard, with technical descent in woodland. Take the 1st gate on the R (ie the one furthest from the barn) and turn sharply R. Follow along LH field edge and through bridlegate into wood. Steeply downhill. You should follow the stream bed but there are alternatives. At road (B4014), L for a mile. At T-j with the A46, R to return to the start.

Route 18

Nailsworth
Horsley
7
6
Kingscote Wood
Kingscote
A46
Wet
Alternative
5
4
Chavenage
Green
A4135
3
Beverston
Tetb
2
N
Radio Mast
8
Wotton-
under-Edge
9
13
Boxwell
10
Newark Park
Ozleworth Bottom
12
Start/Finish
Leighterton
Alderley
A46
11
Tresham
1
Wet
Alternative

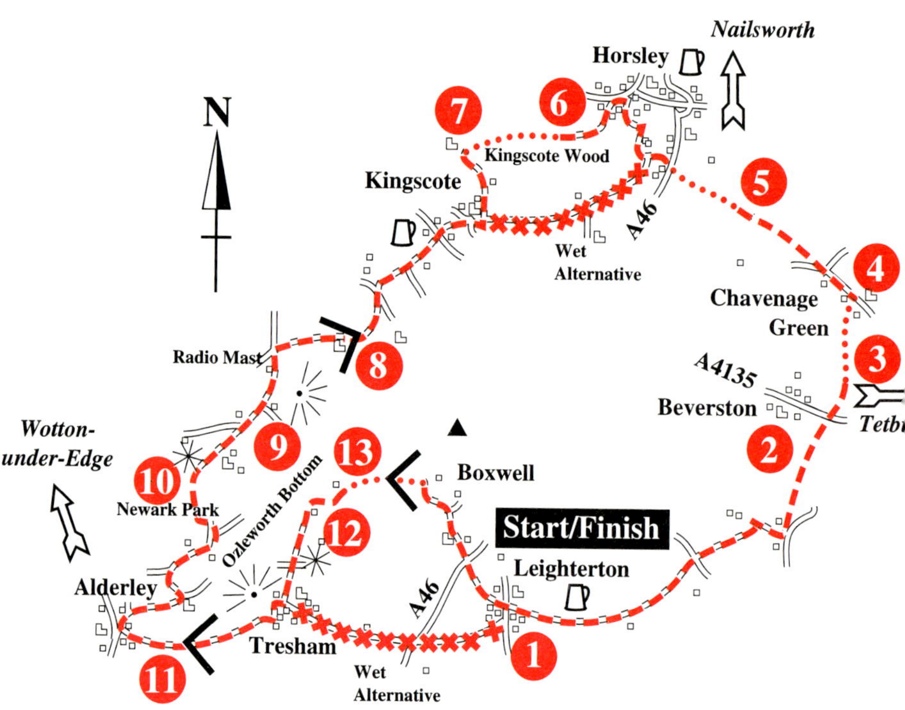

18

Leighterton to Horsley and through Ozleworth Bottom

Distance: 20 miles.
Grade: Moderate/strenuous. (In and out of Ozleworth is strenuous).
Parking: In Leighterton, on the road towards Knockdown and Didmarton, just past church, near the phone box. If you use the Car Park at the Royal Oak PH, please use the pub or at least ask the landlord for permission to park.
Start: The Royal Oak PH, Leighterton, 7 miles south of Nailsworth.
Height gain: 1500 ft.
Main climbs: 400 ft from Horsley to Kingscote, 280 ft beyond Kingscote, near to Ashcroft House, 450 ft from Ozleworth Bottom to Tresham, 280 ft. from Ozleworth Bottom back to Leighterton.
Maps: OS Landranger 162 or Pathfinders 1132 and 1133 for greater detail in the steeply wooded valleys.
Facilities: Pub in Leighterton. Pub and shop in Horsley. (Shop open Sat and Sun AM) Pub in Kingscote. At the crossing point of the A46 above Horsley: Tipputs Inn and a garage which sells chocolate and soft drinks.

This ride shows the two contrasting aspects to offroad cycling in the Cotswolds: the eastern half of the route is fairly flat and open, the western half (the escarpment), steeply wooded, cut through by streams. The ride starts gently along quiet lanes. Fairly flat tracks of varying quality lead north then northwest past Chavenage House to Horsley, the start of the steep, wooded section. You gradually climb alongside a stream up to Kingscote, location of a most splendid hostelry, The Hunters Hall. A sharp climb on road takes you to the mast from where a lovely permitted bridleway gives one of the best descents of the ride. Climb out of the valley to Tresham and gird your loins for another descent, getting technical towards the bottom. The climb back up to Leighterton starts with a very muddy section but improves as it passes the handsome house at Boxwell Court.

Places of interest

Beverston. Scenic village. One of the few surviving Cotswolds castles – largely 13th century with 17th century alterations. Not open to the public but can be glimpsed from near church.

Chavenage House. Fine Elizabethan Manor once visited by Oliver Cromwell. Occasionally open to the public.

Newark Park. Originally a hunting lodge in Elizabethan times. Converted in 1790 into a castellated country house.

Ozleworth. The church has a very rare central hexagonal tower.

1. From the Royal Oak, take the road signposted 'Westonbirt, Tetbury' At x-rds after 2 miles, SA 'Tetbury 3'. After 1 mile, just past Hookshouse Pottery on left, 50 yds past a right turning to Westonbirt, L on to track, passing greenhouses on your left.

2. Keep to RH field edge, then through gate on to green lane. After ¾ mile, as track turns sharp left, continue SA along field edge to join the busy A4135. At main road, R then L on to Public Bridleway.

3. At gate where track ends, go SA downhill into field along the LH field edge. It may be muddy at the bottom and you will have to push uphill anyway as the surface is rough to start with. The track improves near to the farm and Chavenage House.

4. At road, L (or R for 200 yds to see Chavenage House). Ignore the first road on the right. Take the next track/lane on the R. At T-j with another track turn R, then shortly, at fork of bridleways, bear L past house.

5. At x-rds of tracks, SA. Maybe muddy after rain. At the A46 by Tipputs Inn (*), SA, between garage and pub, 'Unsuitable for HGV'. In Horsley, just before Bell and Castle PH, sharply L back on yourself on to 'Bridlepath'.

[*ALTERNATIVE after rain, avoiding mud in Kingscote Wood – at A46, SA on to narrow lane to the left of the garage between stone wall and hedge. At T-j, with a trig point set into the wall ahead, turn R. Follow this road through Kingscote to Hunters Hall Inn on the A4135. Rejoin route at Instruction no. 7 "...L then R, 'Newington 1, Bagpath 1'"].

6. Follow broad track downhill, L past houses and round gate. Gentle uphill on broad track. At fork of tracks by pylon bear L downhill to clearing. Ignore major track to left, continue SA. There may be muddy sections. Exit wood via gate on to the upper, LH, grassy track, following in same direction as it joins a better stony track.

7. At T-j with farm drive near pond, L uphill. Follow through farm to road. At T-j by buildings, R and follow lane to the A4135. At T-j with main road by Hunters Hall Inn, L then R, 'Newington 1, Bagpath 1'.

8. Ignore left turning to Newington. At T-j by triangle of grass, L then R, steeply down then steeply uphill. At T-j near to Communications Tower, L, then at fork by tower itself, L again 'Ozleworth. Newark Park'.

9. After ½ mile, R on track 'Newark Park. National Trust'. At road, SA through iron gates into park. Just before house and cattle grid, R on Permitted Bridleway on to grass then L through wicket gate alongside wall.

10. The narrow rough track soon improves. Follow this wonderful descent right down to the road. Turn R for ½ mile then 1st concrete track L towards and through farm. Follow this track/lane as far as x-rds by cottages and turn L uphill.

11. At times very steep. After 1½ miles, in Tresham, opposite telephone box on the right, turn L (*) uphill on track 'No through road for motor vehicles'. Follow main track towards communications tower, ignoring major footpaths/tracks to right and left. At 1st fork of tracks, R though double red metal gates. At 2nd fork, also at double gates, take the lower, LH track downhill.

[*ALTERNATIVE/SHORT CUT avoiding mud after rain in Ozleworth Bottom. Do not turn L, go SA to A46, turn L then 1st R 'Leighterton' to return to start].

12. This becomes a sunken track which passes through several gates, including two by a lovely old Cotswold farmhouse. Continue in the same direction on tarmac down to a stream.

13. Do not cross the stream but bear slightly R on to muddy track. The first bit is the worst. Stay on upper track passing above the fine old house of Boxwell, with the perimeter wall to your left. At the end of the wall, head for the grey barn then at tarmac SA. At x-rds with the A46, SA and into Leighterton to return to start.

Route 19

Cirencester
5
South
Cerney
A419 (M4)
N
Dismantled Railway
4
Start/Finish
Car Park
1
Cotswold
Water Park
3
Hailstone Hill
Ashton Keynes
Derry Brook
2
Waterhay

19

Cotswold Water Park

Distance: 9 miles.
Grade: Easy (the easiest in the book).
Parking: Car Park on the B4696 south of South Cerney (GR SU 052952).
Start: As above.
Height gain: Almost nothing.
Maps: OS Landranger 163.
Facilities: Pubs and shops in South Cerney.

This route was essentially devised by the wardens at the Cotswold Water Park who have done a splendid job managing an ever changing asset (new gravel pits are constantly being dug and the course of rights of way diverted.) The route takes you among some of the many lakes formed by gravel extraction, is well signposted and over good surfaces, including a section of dismantled railway. Amongst the other curiosities you may see, keep an eye out for a street in South Cerney by the bridge called 'Bow Wow'!

Places of interest

South Cerney. 18th century octagonal gazebo by the River Churn. Many fine houses in Church Lane and Silver Street.

1. Follow signs for 'Bridlepath Circuit. South Cerney, Cricklade' then over motorbike barrier 'Waterhay 1½ miles'. Follow round field edge parallel to road. At tarmac, SA over motorbike barrier on to Public Bridleway 'Waterhay ¾ mile'. Shortly, cross road 'Waterhay ½ mile' (Blue arrow).

2. Do not be tempted into the quicksand! Follow the fence round to the L with its myriad quicksand signs 'Public Bridleway. Cricklade 3 miles'. With gate ahead on to 'Private Road', turn R over small wooden bridge over stream. After 200 yds, at T-j of tracks beyond motorbike barrier, L 'Public Bridleway. South Cerney 2½ miles'.

3. Follow signs for South Cerney. Keep your eye out for a gap in the line of trees on your right to join a better parallel track which is the old dismantled railway. Follow this under a bridge. At junction with the (busy) B4696, SA beneath redbrick railway bridges.

4. Follow to next road, turn L for 200 yds, then on LH bend, just past 'South Cerney' sign, opposite double green metal gates, R through bridle gate (blue arrow). Go past housing estate into countryside. At road, L into South Cerney. (Keep a look out for a lane just before the Old George Inn called Bow Wow !!)

5. At T-j, R 'Ewen, Ashton Keynes' then after 100 yds, L by memorial cross on Broadway Lane. At the end of Broadway Lane, R 'Ashton Keynes, Somerford Keynes' for 1 mile to return to car park 'Picnic Site'.

Route 20

N
Castle Combe
Start/Finish
Wet Alternative
B4039
1
10
3
2
9
North Wraxall
A420
West Yatton
Chippenham
Bristol
8
Biddestone
By Brook
7
Thickwood
4
Colerne
6
5

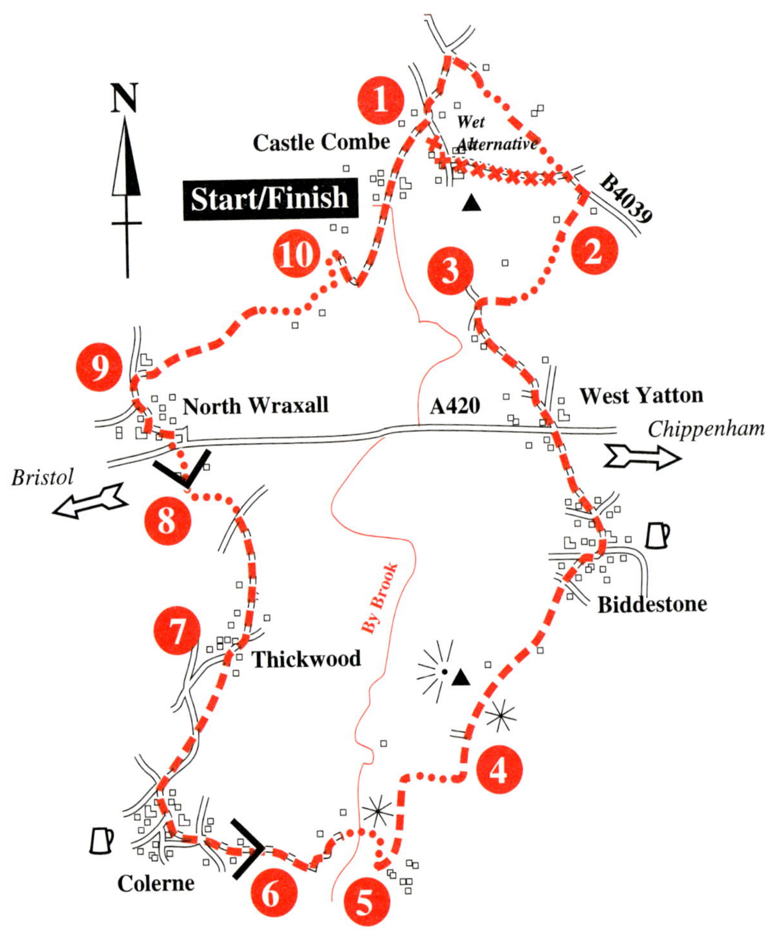

20

From Castle Combe to small villages in the southern Cotswolds

Distance: 15 miles.
Grade: Moderate.
Parking: Car park at top of Castle Combe just off the B4039.
Start: From the car park.
Height gain: 1100 ft.
Main climbs: 350 ft from By Brook up to Colerne. 200 ft into North Wraxall.
Maps: OS Landranger 173.
Facilities: Lots in Castle Combe. 2 pubs in Biddestone. Shop and pub in Colerne.

Leaving exploration of Castle Combe until the end of the ride, the route follows byways then bridleways south to the attractive village of Biddestone where the village pond used to have a ducking stool. An easy track with good views soon turns to a faster descent, possibly ending in mud! A climb out of the valley sets you up for another downhill, at times technical, to cross the By Brook. You may well set your lungs on fire climbing into Colerne! Enjoy a flatter section before diving down into the woods again near to North Wraxall. The next climb is a steep push to the A420. A final wooded section beyond Truckle Hill leaves you poised for the swoop down into Castle Combe. If you have brought a change of clothes they may even let you into a tea shop for a well deserved cream tea blow out!

Places of interest

Castle Combe. Grew around the weaving trade. The last mills were pulled down in 1820. In 1947 the whole village was put up for sale by the Lord of the Manor and the Manor House became a hotel. In 1962, Castle Combe was voted the prettiest village in England, the tourists started arriving in droves and they haven't stopped! In 1966 it was chosen as location for the film production of 'The Story of Doctor Doolittle'.

Biddestone, Colerne, North Wraxall – scenic villages.

1. From the Car Park in Castle Combe, turn L uphill then L (*) at T-j with the B4039. 1st R after 50 yds 'Grittleton 2'. After ½ mile, opposite 1st road on left, R on track 'By Way'. This may be muddy in parts. At road, R then after 150 yds, on RH bend, L 'By Way'. Again, a muddy middle section. At B4039, L. Ignore 1st R to Castle Combe Circuit. Take next track on R.

[*ALTERNATIVE after wet weather: turn R at T-j with the B4039. After 1¼ miles, just after going under power lines (pylons), ignore 1st right to 'Skid Pan Karts' (Castle Combe Circuit). Take next R through metal gate towards farmhouse set back from road. Rejoin route at instruction no. 2].

2. Follow past farm and through metal gate into enclosed green track which deteriorates then improves. In field, follow RH edge. At gate at end of wood, bear R on upper track parallel with valley floor to your left.

3. At road, L. After a mile, at A420, SA past Crown Inn towards Biddestone. At T-j, R 'Corsham'. After ¼ mile, on sharp LH bend, before the village pond, R along Church Road 'Hartham'. After ½ mile. on sharp LH bend as road changes name to 'Hartham Lane', go SA on to Weavern Lane No Through Road'.

4. Where tarmac ends at fork, take LH (lower) track. Just BEFORE gate with 'Private Woods' sign, L downhill. The lowest section may be muddy. Start climbing. At x-rds of tracks, SA uphill on narrower track, keeping barbed wire on your right. At T-j with more major track, L uphill towards pylon.

5. Go past farm. On sharp LH bend, with two houses ahead of you, R downhill on track. Shortly, with metal gates either side, continue downhill and to the right on narrow track. Technical in parts. At bottom, bear R on broad track. At two houses, turn L and at T-j beyond gate, L towards barns.

6. Steep climb. At x-rds, R towards church. Just past church, R past bus shelter then R again on Quarry Lane. At x-rds, R 'Chippenham, Ford'. After ¼ mile at start of sweeping LH bend, R on to grassy track 'Thickwood. Bridleway'. This narrows then widens. At T-j with road, R.

7. Ignore 1st left by the telephone box. Take next L opposite a sign for 'Euridge, Colerne'. At 1st T-j, L. At 2nd T-j with more major road, SA through metal gate 'Bridleway'. Follow along RH field edge into wood. Ignore 1st right downhill. Keep to LH edge of wood. Leave main track on next track R downhill. Small green sign on tree 'Public Path'.

8. Fork R again to continue steeply downhill (muddy). Cross stream and climb steeply. At A420, SA on to track. At minor lane, L downhill into

108

North Wraxall. Turn R by church 'Nettleton, Castle Combe, West Kington'.

9. After ¼ mile, just before large grey barn on your right, R on No Through Road (tarmac). Through green gate on to track. At recently converted house, turn L, leaving main track (blue arrow on stout post) through two gates in same direction around field edge. At bottom corner of field, L through gate to continue downhill.

10. Cross stream and climb to road junction. Take the road downhill into Castle Combe. Through Castle Combe, up hill and 1st L 'Acton Turville 4, B4039' to return to car park.

Route 21

Banbury
Epwell
9
8
Iron Age
Hill Fort
Blenheim
Farm
7
B4035
Madmarston
Hill
Wet Alternative
6
10
B4035
Ditchedge Lane
Swalcliffe
5
3
N
Traitor's
Ford
4
11
Nill Farm
2
Brewery
Hook Norton
Start/Finish
12
1

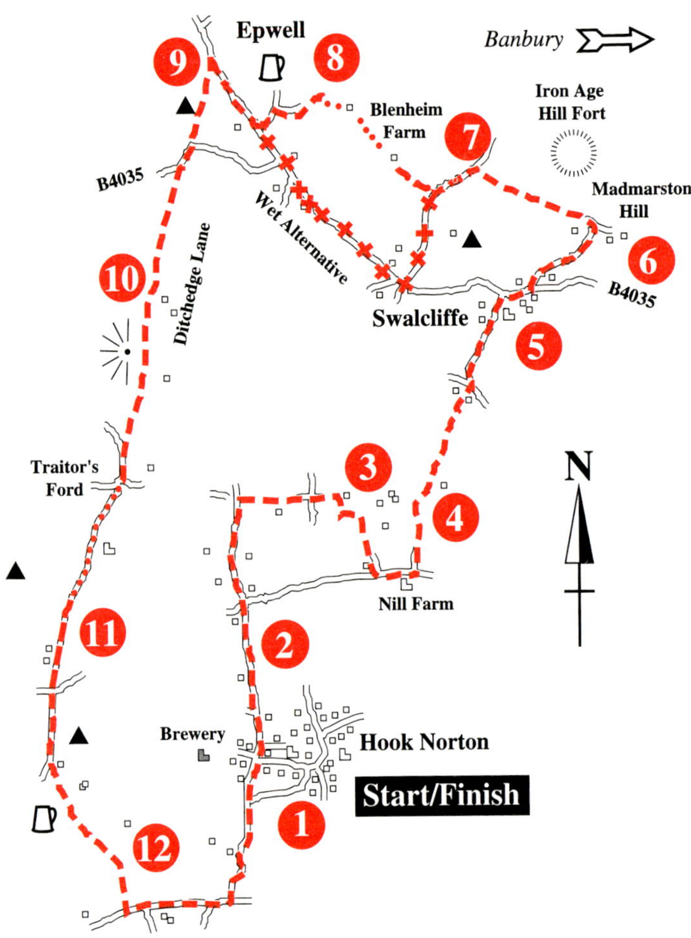

21
Hook Norton to the ridge track on the Warwickshire/Oxfordshire boundary

Distance: 17 miles.
Grade: Moderate.
Parking: No specific car park, show consideration.
Start: The church, Hook Norton, 6 miles northeast of Chipping Norton.
Height gain: 900 ft.
Main climbs: 250 ft from below Madmarston Hill to the mast on Ditchledge Lane, 430 ft from Traitor's Ford to the mast by Whichford Hill Farm.
Maps: OS Landranger 151.
Facilities: Shops, pubs in Hook Norton. Pub in Swalcliffe. (Pubs in Epwell, Great Rollright, Sibford Gower, just off the route).

Hook Norton is famous for its very fine ales and a pilgrimage to have a look at the brewery, even if only from the outside, is well worthwhile. The ride wends its way north through rolling farmland, into Swalcliffe and beneath an Iron Age Fort on Madmarston Hill. At this point you are on a section of Roman Road that doesn't obviously link up with any other section. Perhaps they were just practising. All is going fine and dandy until you get beyond Blenheim Farm and you are faced with just over ½ mile of open fields. Miserable if muddy. (Wet weather alternative suggested). Fear not! You soon reach the start of Ditchledge Lane, the Warwickshire/Oxfordshire boundary that you follow offroad and on road for the next 5½ miles. Fine views in both directions, although the descent to Traitor's Ford is bumpy rather than fast. Wind those legs up for a 430 ft climb to the next mast, and it is mainly downhill from there back to the start.

Places of interest

Hook Norton. Used to yield great quantities of ironstone, it now yields great quantities of very fine beer, brewed at the unlikely looking Victorian red brick building at the western end of the village (along Brewery Lane from near the Pear Tree PH). The font in the church is unusual for its sculptured figures of Sagittarius the Archer and other signs of the Zodiac.

Another nearby curiosity is the huge dismantled railway viaduct that used to carry the Banbury and Cheltenham Direct Railway. (It lies to the southeast of the village).

Swalcliffe. Fine Tithe Barn.

1. With your back to church, turn R out of village along a road that changes name from High St to Netting St to Scotland End. At a triangle of grass at the bottom of a hill, by the Pear Tree Inn, turn R 'Sibford Gower'.

2. At x-rds, SA 'Sibford Gower'. 300 yds past Jack and Jill Nursery, halfway down a long hill, opposite a road turning on your left, turn R on to Public Bridleway 'Swalcliffe'. At road, SA over cattlegrid 'Swalcliffe'.

3. Follow this main track as it bends R then L towards the farm. Just before a '20 mph' sign, by some large round metal tanks on your left, turn R on to tarmac and follow this farm drive to the road. At road, L for 400 yds then L on track opposite the Atcost barns on the right.

4. Follow this track for 1½ miles to road. At road, L then R 'Swalcliffe'.

5. At T-j, R into Swalcliffe then 1st L after church 'Swalcliffe Lea'.

6. After ¾ mile, shortly after passing isolated farm with redbrick tin-roofed garages on left, take first track L (broad, stone-based) on a sharp RH bend. (Iron Age Fort above and to your right). Follow this good stony track to the road.

7. At road, L for ½ mile, dropping then climbing a short hill. Take the first track R, (*) 'Blenheim Farm', 'Bridleway, Epwell'. Follow tarmac to the end, leaving all buildings to your right. At end of tarmac, continue SA on broad stony track along RH field edge. After 200 yds, as main track swings sharply left downhill, SA across field.

8. WARNING! The next ½ mile section may be very muddy in winter/after rain and rough in the summer. At the hedgerow, R for 50 yds then L through a wooden gate into a grassy pasture and head for the next farm.

[*ALTERNATIVE after rain – Do NOT turn R to Blenheim Farm, follow road to x-rds with B4035, turn R for 1¼ miles, then on sharp LH bend, bear R (in effect SA), 'Epwell'. After a mile, after footpath signs to right and left, L on major track. Rejoin at Instruction no. 10 'This heads back....'].

9. Go past farm, jinking L through green gates on to main track which you follow to the road. At road, L then after 50 yds, at T-j, turn R 'Tysoe 3'.

Excellent stone bridleway near Dartley Farm, south of Woodmancote

10. After ½ mile, after passing footpath on left and right, take the first track L 'Bridleway'. (This heads back towards the mast you have seen on your left). At road, R then at the 'Warwickshire' sign, L on to the track.

11. Lovely ridge track with good views in both directions. This becomes a rough grassy track as it descends to the stream at Traitor's Ford. At the road, L through the ford and be prepared for a 430 ft climb, divided into three stages, following signs for Great Rollright.

12. At x-rds, SA 'Great Rollright. Chipping Norton'. Shortly after passing radio tower on left, take the next lane/track on L 'Court Farm'. Leave tarmac as it turns left towards first farm. Carry SA on LH field edge.

13. At sign for Berry Field Farm, bear R on better track to road. Turn L on road to return to Hook Norton.

Route 22

N
Rollright Stones
6
LIttle Compton
Chastleton Hill
7
Over Norton
Salford
A436
A44
2
1
5
3
Chipping Norton
Daylesford
Wet Alternative
Start/Finish
4
Kingham

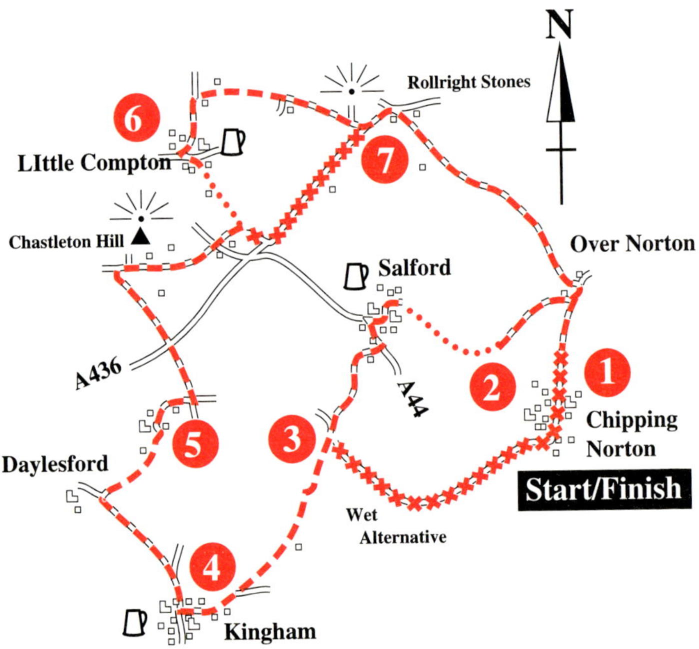

22
Chipping Norton, three counties and The Rollright Stones

Distance: 18 miles.
Grade: Moderate.
Parking: Follow signs to free parking on Albion Street, parallel with the High Street.
Start: White Hart Hotel, High Street, Chipping Norton.
Height gain: 1200 ft.
Main climbs: 350 ft from Daylesford to Chastleton Hill, 300 ft from Little Compton on to the Rollright ridge and 300 ft of climbing back into Chipping Norton from Rollright.
Maps: OS Landranger 151, 163, 164 or Pathfinder 1044, 1068.
Facilities: Lots in Chipping Norton. Pubs in Salford, Kingham and Little Compton.

Starting in Chipping Norton, Oxfordshire, this ride dips into Gloucestershire and Warwickshire as it heads west then north. It also crosses parts of three OS Landranger maps (or two Pathfinder maps), but with any luck the instructions should be clear enough for you not to need to refer to them too frequently. A stiff climb to Over Norton finds you at the start of a good track that deteriorates, although it is downhill. After Salford, better offroad tracks take you into Kingham then up the hill from Daylesford to Chastleton. Views to the north start opening up. Down and up from Little Compton. Time for a culture stop! The Rollright Stones are no Stonehenge but atmospheric none the less, placed on top of the ridge with views in both directions. Well stoned, it's time for the last descent then climb back to the start.

Places of interest

Chipping Norton. The long market square or 'chepynge' as it was known in the Middle Ages (hence 'Chipping' from which 'shopping' is derived) is dominated by the 19th century Town Hall. The town used to be on a major coaching route and many of the hotels and inns date back to those times

Rollright Stones. Bronze Age (c.2000 BC) stone circle a hundred feet in diameter. The ridge on which they stand is believed to have carried the 'Jurassic Way' leading southwest along the limestone belt from the shores of the Humber to Salisbury Plain and the coast beyond. The 18th century historian, William Stukeley referred to the stones as being 'corroded like worm-eaten wood by the harsh jaws of time'. (No, he wasn't referring to Keith Richards.)

Kingham, Daylesford and Chastleton all boast splendid old houses. Only Chastleton is open to the public.

1. With back to the White Hart Hotel, R (*) to the mini-roundabout at the end of the High Street, bear L on the B4026 Over Norton Road 'Over Norton, Great Rollright'. At top of short steep hill, on sharp RH bend, L on Cleeves Corner. Ignore right turn towards barn after ¼ mile.

[*ALTERNATIVE avoiding rough track between Over Norton and Salford. From the White Hart Hotel, L to the small roundabout near the Town Hall, take the B4450 towards Churchill, Bledington, Stow-on-the-Wold for 1½ miles then 1st R at offset x-rds, 'Kingham Hill School, Cornwell'. After 1½ mile, just after crossing bridges over disused railway then river, L on track. 'Kingham 2' Rejoin route at Instruction no. 3 '..Good quality track..'].

2. As main track sweeps left uphill, bear R towards copse. The surface deteriorates after the copse and may be muddy or rutted, but it is basically downhill. At end of copse, SA along LH edge of field ahead. Join tarmac at Salford and follow in the same direction until The Black Horse PH. Turn L just before the bus shelter and at the main road ((A44), L then 1st R 'Cornwell 1¾'.

3. After 1 mile, at T-j, L 'Chipping Norton, Churchill' then after 150 yds 1st track R 'Bridleway. Kingham 2' (Blue arrow). Good quality track. At tarmac, bear L (in effect SA) then after 200 yds, on sharp LH bend, bear R (in effect SA) on to track. At road, R.

4. At x-rds in Kingham (Plough Inn), R 'Daylesford, Cornwell' then 1st L after ¼ mile 'Daylesford, Stow-on-the-Wold'. After 1½ miles, by the first telegraph pole, R on to track. Gentle climb. Follow wall round to the left past a plant nursery. At x-rds of tracks by a large new building/barn, turn L towards wood, then at the end of the barn, turn R.

5. At road, R then at x-rds after ½ mile, L 'Chastleton'. At x-rds with A436, SA 'Chastleton 1½'. After 1½ miles, on sharp LH bend, 1st R 'The

Rollrights' 'Unfenced road' 'Private Property. No camping'. Fine views to the left. At A44, SA through farmyard and carry on in the same direction as tarmac turns to grassy track. At double red metal gates, (*) L alongside wall. At times rough/muddy with badger sets.

[*ALTERNATIVE after rain, or short cut – at double red gates, R to road. At road, L for 2 miles to Rollright Stones and x-rds for return to Chipping Norton. Rejoin route at instruction no.7 '...R, Little Rollright ½,...'].

6. At road, L, then 2nd road on R 'Reed College' 'To the church'. Follow past the church then 1st L 'Barton on the Heath 1½'. Ignore right to Hawton Farm. At top of short hill, turn R on broad track towards farm (blue arrow on yellow circle). Follow in the same direction, crossing to the other side of the fence/hedgerow at barns. Leave these to your left and follow track uphill along RH edge of field on other side of metal gate. At T-j of tracks, R towards masts. At road, L.

7. At T-j with next road, L 'Rollright Stones, Great Rollright 2½' then at x-rds, SA to see Rollright Stones, OR, for continuation of route, R 'Little Rollright ½, Chipping Norton 3½'. Halfway up the hill, 1st R 'Over Norton'. At T-j in Over Norton, R 'Chipping Norton 1'.

Route 23

Start/Finish
Great Tew
Chipping Norton
Little Tew
Banbury
1
B4022
Ford
N
Airfield
2
B4022
Enstone
B4030
Gagingwell
4
3
Cleveley
River Glyme

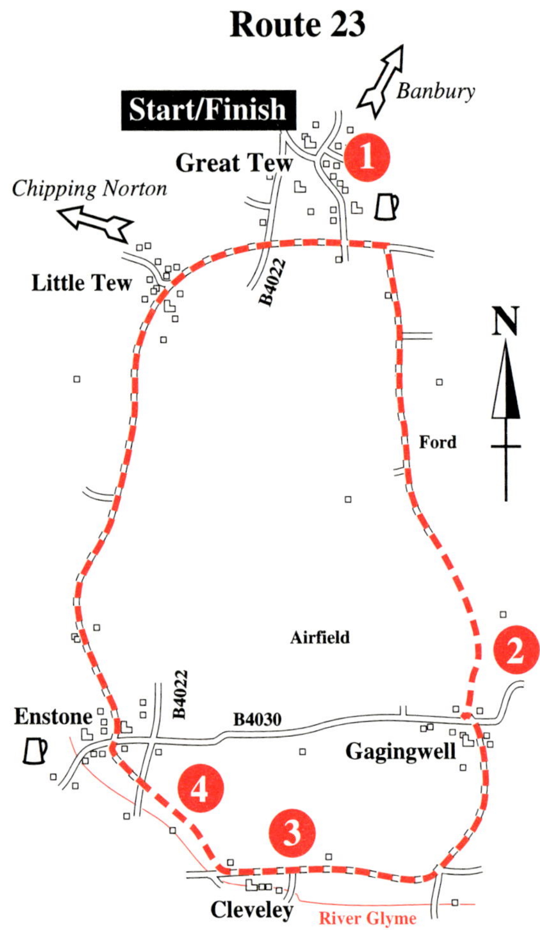

23

Easy tracks and quiet lanes near Great Tew

Distance: 10 miles.
Grade: Easy.
Parking: Car Park in Great Tew by a grey telephone box.
Start: Post Office, Great Tew, 7 miles northeast of Chipping Norton.
Height gain: 250 ft.
Main climbs: None to worry about.
Maps: OS Landranger 164.
Facilities: Pub and tea shop/store in Great Tew. Pub in Church Enstone.

Great Tew is a little gem of a village, until recently in a spiralling decline through neglect. Many houses have since been renovated and the character of the place has changed dramatically. The route is short and easy, passing the Manor House in Great Tew, taking a No Through Road leading to a pair of farms and down into a ford. Skirting the airfield northeast of Enstone, the ride proceeds on tiny lanes to Cleveley for a delightful short section by the upper River Glyme. Climbing out of the valley, you pass through Little Tew before returning to the start. There is a short section of bridleway north of Great Tew that is worth exploring, although it does not lead on to any other offroad section of note. (Indeed I tried SIX different bridleways/unclassified roads branching off this track to make a second loop, all without success, each ending in thick mud, dense vegetation, severely rutted tracks or a combination of all three....).

Places of interest

Great Tew. A model village created in the early 19th century by the landscape gardner John Loudon as part of an extensive park overlooking the Worton Valley. It is for this reason that there are so many evergreen trees in the vicinity.

1. With your back to the Post Office in Great Tew, go SA uphill towards the triangle of grass with a wooden bench. Turn L (towards church, the

Bartons). At T-j by triangle of grass and post box, turn L then 1st road to the R after 300 yds 'Tracey and Beaconsfield Farms only'.

2. Follow this lane/track in the same direction, ignoring turns to the left then right. After 1¼ miles you have a chance to go ford busting. ¾ mile after the ford, at a T-j with a concrete track, turn L for 50 yds then at offset x-rds of tracks, SA on track leading between fields towards a line of trees. Follow it to its end as it veers sharply R.

3. After 20 yds turn L through the bridle gate and along the LH edge of a field (the aerodrome is to your right). Follow in the same direction, IGNORE the first field gate on your left, take the more distant one to continue to the road. Emerge by 'The Old Farm' and turn L. After 200 yds, R 'Radford'. After a mile, at x-rds, R 'Cleveley 1¼'

4. After another mile, at sharp LH bend downhill, with a bridleway coming in from the right, bear slightly right (in effect SA) 'Bridleway' (blue arrow). Keep bearing L downhill. Cross stream and turn R. Emerge at tarmac. By a triangle of grass, turn R 'Public bridleway. Church Enstone 1' (This section may be overgrown).

5. At road, SA 'Unsuitable for HGV'. At T-j in Enstone, L for refreshments at Crown Inn, OR, for continuation of route, R then L 'Little Tew 2½'. At T-j in Little Tew, R 'Great Tew 1¼'. At B4022, SA 'Ledwell, Duns Tew'. After ½ mile 1st L to return to Great Tew.

Route 24

Chipping Norton
B4026
8
9
N
Chadlington
7
Ditchley Park
Charlbury
10
6
Start/Finish
1
B4437
River Evenlode
Wychwood Forest
Stonesfield
5
Leafield
2
Akeman Street Roman Road
3
North Leigh
4
Witney

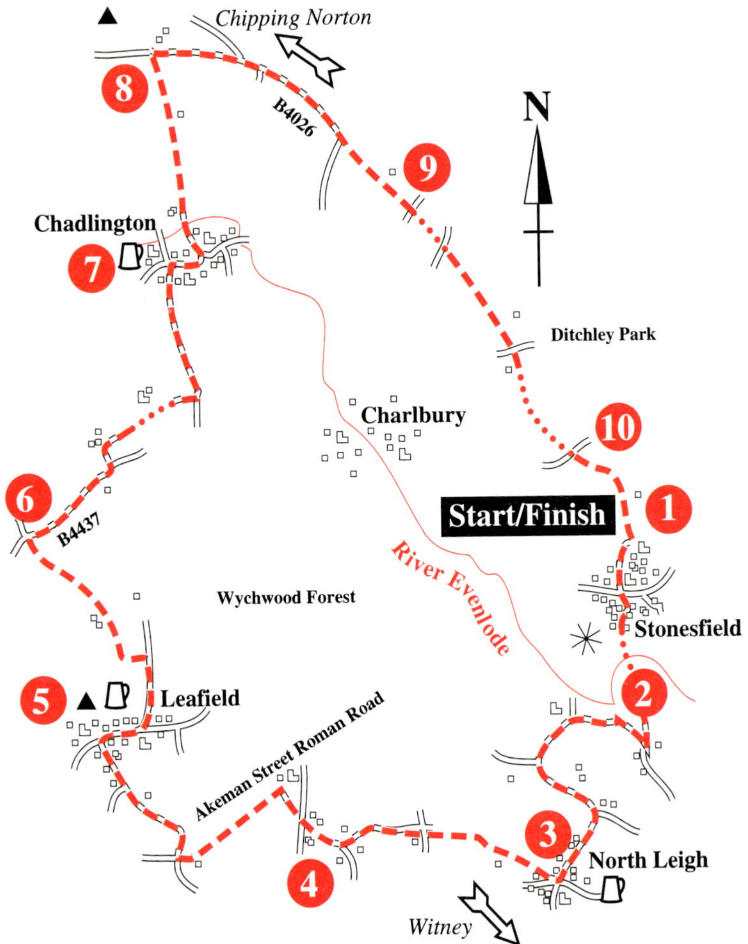

24

In and out of the Evenlode valley from Stonesfield

Distance: 24 miles.
Grade: Moderate.
Parking: No specific parking in the village so please act with consideration. There is a large car park at the back of the White Horse PH which you must ask to use and/or stop for a drink. Do not abuse this.
Start: The Black Head PH, Stonesfield, 5 miles northeast of Witney.
Height gain: 1100 ft.
Main climbs: Several climbs between 100 ft and 200 ft. From Evenlode valley north through Chadlington – 350 ft.
Maps: OS Landranger 164.
Facilities: Pubs and shop in Stonesfield. Pubs in North Leigh, Leafield, Chadlington.

This long, rambling ride describes a wide circle around Charlbury at the eastern side of the Cotswolds. It links several small villages via bridleways, disused county roads, a section of an old Roman road (Akeman Street near Leafield) and long stretches of RUPPs (roads used as public paths). Its linking theme is the River Evenlode and the valley it forms. Risng near Moreton-in-Marsh, it joins the Thames at Eynsham cutting through the Oolithic Limestone to form a valley steep enough to give this ride a technical section right at its start where you drop down from Stonesfield .

Places of interest

Stonesfield. Centre for Cotswold slate. Lock up near the church.

North Leigh Roman Villa. Situated near the banks of the River Evenlode are the remains of a large 4th century Roman Villa on a site first occupied in the 1st century. Initially excavated in 1813, these remains surround a courtyard and include living quarters with mosaics and a bath.

Wychwood Forest. From Saxon times this was a royal forest with the great hunting lodge at Woodstock. Every king from Ethelred the Unready to

James 1 visited the forest. During the 19th century the great woodlands were split up into several parks and much was cleared for farming.

Chadlington. Fine 17th century manor house. Many curious gargoyles on the outside of the church.

Grim's Ditch (near Ditchley Park). Series of banks and ditches that once formed part of a defensive system built by a 1st century Iron Age tribe.

Akeman Street (south of Leafield). Roman Road that used to run from Cirencester to St Albans via Bicester.

1. With your back to the Black Head PH, L along Church Street. At the end of the lane, SA on to Brook Lane 'Oxfordshire Way'. Technical descent! Cross the River Evenlode via the bridge and continue in the same direction across a field (maybe muddy) towards next gate.

2. Climb on better track to road. Turn R on road, then at x-rds, L 'North Leigh, Witney'. Ignore 1st right by large triangle of grass. Just after a small stone built house, take the next R on Church Road 'North Leigh, Witney' (Masons Arms PH, Windmill in North Leigh).

3. At T-j with New Yatt Way, R then 1st R after the Woodman PH on to Green Lane. Follow the tarmac lane. Shortly after passing low farm buildings then a house called 'Home Close' on your left, leave the tarmac lane on a sharp RH bend, bearing L on to track. At T-j with next tarmac track, L.

4. At x-rds, SA 'Delly End, Hailey' then 1st R 'Oak Tree Nur(series)'. At T-j, L and on sharp LH bend by sign for Wood Lane, R on to track. Just beyond old sheds, bear R through hedge on to better parallel track continuing in the same direction. At the end of 'Singe Wood', at junction with the B4022, SA on to track. After ½ mile, just before large farm and tall deciduous trees, L on major track. As this track turns sharp left, go SA along the RH field edge by a fence. At tarmac, R on minor road.

5. At T-j, R 'Leafield, Shipton'. At next T-j, by the church in Leafield, R then after ½ mile, 1st L 'Chadlington'. At the bottom of the hill, just as the wood begins on the right, L on track (blue arrow). Good stony track.

6. At road, R for 1 mile then 1st L, 'Chilson'. In Chilson, 50 yds after telephone box on left, R on bridleway 'Oxfordshire Way'. Follow to tarmac, ignore left turns on minor lanes, go SA for ½ mile to T-j with more major road, turn L downhill to cross River Evenlode and climb into Chadlington.

7. At T-j in Chadlington, R 'Dean, Spelsbury', then 1st L on to Church Road just after Chadlington House Hotel. (Malt Shovel PH lies SA after hotel). On a sharp LH bend by Chadlington Bowling Club, bear R (in effect SA) on to track. Good stony track climbing gently for 1½ miles as far as road.

8. At T-j with road, R then at next T-j, with B4026, R for just over a mile. Ignore turning to left to Lidstone, Enstone. On a sharp RH bend with chevrons and a 'RH bend' sign, bear L on to track 'Right of Way'.

9. Follow good broad track in same direction SA at minor road then SA at major road (B4022). This short ½ mile section may be rough. At T-j with tarmac at the edge of the wood, turn L. The track becomes rougher. Go past the twin white lodges of Ditchley Park. As the track bears right towards farm just after the start of a wooden fence on the right, bear L (in effect SA) on to broad grassy track along LH field edge. (Becomes rougher).

10. At road (B4437), SA along field edge. Through gate, leaving farm and dovecotes on your left. Good grassy then stone track to road. At road, R into Stonesfield, turning L by the White Horse PH, 'Combe, Woodstock'. After the shops, on sharp LH bend, R on Church St to return to start.

25
The Forest of Dean

Although no specific route is described here, it is certainly worth mentioning the area as there are few places in Southern England that have adopted as liberal a policy as the Forestry Commission in the Forest of Dean. With the exception of three small areas which are for exclusive use of walkers, there is an 'open access' policy for mountain bikes on the forestry tracks that go through the woodlands owned by the Forestry Commission.

The best way to appreciate the Forest of Dean is to turn up with a compass, some food and drink and the Ordnance Survey Outdoor Leisure map no. 14 'Wye Valley and Forest of Dean', park in any of the many car parks in the Forest and make up your own routes. Although at times you may not know exactly where you are, it is very hard to get 'lost' as you are at no stage more than two miles from a road which you can either use to get your bearings or follow back to your start point.

The fine hostelry in Great Tew

FALKLAND ARMS
Great Tew